Dad's

*100 Poems, Riddles,
and Songs in 100 Days*

Jeffrey Krueger

Copyright © 2022 by Jeffrey Krueger

All rights reserved. No part of this book may be reproduced or transmitted in any form or by any means, electronic or mechanical, including photocopying, recording, or any information storage and retrieval system, without permission in writing from the author.

ISBN: 979-8-9870661-1-9 - Hardcover
ISBN: 979-8-9870661-0-2 - Paperback
eISBN: 979-8-9870661-2-6 - eBook

Library of Congress Control Number: 2022918395

∞ This paper meets the requirements of ANSI/NISO Z39.48-1992 (Permanence of Paper)

060524

*Dedicated to
Roy Francis Krueger
My wife and beautiful children*

Acknowledgments

I must thank my entire family, especially my wife, for putting up with me through all the readings they endured while I was creating. I give special thanks to my best friend, Bryan O, who listened and read every one of my poems over the hundred days they were created.

To those of you who may purchase this book as a donation to help families in need at the Family Needs Fund charitable event or at your local bookstore or as an eBook, thank you.

To my wife, children, grandchildren, and friends: I hope you enjoy these simple rhyming poems. Hopefully, these rhymes will inspire you. My desire is that this book of poems will be read on certain occasions, connecting us with our love for each other.

Contents

Introduction	*xiii*
About the Poems, Riddles, and Songs	*xv*

Poems:

Autumn Sleep	1
Daydream	2
Another Day	4
Politics	6
Eternity	7
Deep Inside	8
Sadness	9
Skating	11
Seated Reflection	12
Run-Of-The-Mill	13
Graduation	14
Morning Coffee	15
Revealed	16
Magnificent Day	17
The Table	19
Family Gathers	20
Terri	21
New Life	22
Inspiration	24
Poles & Buckets	25
My Love	26
Moving In	27
Echoes	28

Yellow Fellow	29
Lost and Found	31
The Present	33
Trust	34
Happy	36
Bully	38
A Sign	39
At First Sight	40
Fluffy White	42
Divorced Child	44
Keep On Smiling	45
Risen	47
#2	49
Bow Wow	51
Friends	52
Angel's Touch	54
Alive	55
A Face	56
The Choice	57
Whatever/Seriously	58
Simple Pleasure	60
Origination	62
Guardians Spear	63
#1	64
It Conquers All	66
Popped	67
Oh, Hold Me Tight	68
I CAN SEE	70
Precious Gifts	72
Timeless	74
Shadows Conquered	76
French Word	78
Snapped	79
Day by Day	80
A Child's Wound	82

The Harvest	83
A Delight	85
Ring the Bell	87
Countless Treasures	89
MDD	91
Meal for Two	92
The Little Tree	94
The Hunt	96
Oh Daddy, Oh Daddy	98
Contagious	100
I Want to Know	102
Christ the Jesus Emmanuel	103
Justified Nonsense	104
So Precious	105
A Joyous Manuscript	107
Second-Go-Around	109
Riddle of One	111
My Favorite	112
High Above	114
Breaking Free	115
A New	117
Spongy	118
Choice	119
The Designer	120
Our Home	121
Two Left Feet	123
WAR	124
Frosting	125
Deep in the Hole	126
The Gathering	127
The Embrace	128
Blue, Blue, Gray, Gray, White, White, Black	130
May the Light Be with You	131
Coming to Town	132
Fucanglong	134

Citadel Homecoming	136
Preparing	137
Wounded	138
The Week Before	140
Brightly Lit	141
Free Flow	143
Partners	144
To Talk	145
New Normal	147
Falling Flakes	149
Conflict	150
Counselor Comforter	151
It's Not a Compromise	153
Delicious	154
A Deep Breath	156
Gift or Curse	157
Enivid Nommoc Esnes	158
Finish Line	159
Roy Francis Krueger's Poems	*161*

Introduction

Part of my mission for writing these poems was to extend a legacy my father started. Here's a brief part of the story of creating Dad's 100 Poems, Riddles, and Songs in 100 Days.

After fifty-plus years of being in the entertainment business and twenty-eight years at the helm of WE Fest, a country music festival I created in 1983, I finally decided to retire from my controlled chaos. In the pursuing years, I picked up a consulting contract with a small business in Detroit Lakes. I continued to work on a fundraiser for the Family Needs Fund, a nonprofit organization I initiated, designed, and dedicated to assisting the crisis and circumstantial needs of families. It's still active today, thank you, Bo.

I became involved with consulting a small Christian music fest called Hope Fest, a fundraiser for the homeless, hungry, and lost. I decided at my retirement that this was also a good time to get back to my drawings and to attempt writing a bit. I started my first writing adventure because I wanted to prove to myself that I could overcome my writing and spelling incapability, or now called learning difference.

I had to challenge myself since I was made fun of in my early school years. I couldn't spell or pronounce certain words because I was mildly dyslexic and was reluctant to read out loud. I missed the second- and third-grade basic English studies because of my family's dysfunction. I blamed some of my learning disorder on those two early years. Surely not the total reason but it didn't help in adding to my mental acuity.

I had an idea for a movie, and I thought maybe I could write the screenplay. That was my first attempt. I went on to finish my screenplay, called **The Maestro**, *about a young boy who saves the world through his healing music. I started my autobiography, of which I'm halfway finished. I consider myself a devoted husband, father, and grandfather to my four children and nine grandchildren. Believe it or not, I also became a full-time farmer and reclaimed-wood-furniture-maker and inventor.*

When I got stuck in manufacturing this year (2021) with my E-Z Stack invention (e-zstack.com), I needed to take a break. So, I went back to writing. Now I had a new challenge to write 100 poems, riddles, and songs in 100 days. It was a crazy idea since I only had written several poems prior, but I thought what the heck. *If anything, it would be a fun journey of creativity.*

The whole concept became even more interesting when I talked to my brother. Now my added mission is to complete a generational legacy. After emailing a few poems to him to see what he thought, he replied by saying, "Don't quit your day job."

I said, "I don't have a day job." He continued telling me the story of our father boasting about how he was going to finish a book of poems and make a lot of money to take care of us. I was rather moved by the discontent in my brother's voice.

In my autobiography, I explained the difficult journey my father had with his alcohol and sickness. He could barely keep a job, let alone write a book of poems. I explained to my brother that I have several of dad's poems and maybe I'll figure out some meaningful way to pass them on.

So, I thought, I'm going to finish what my dad started. *Beginning with* Dad's 100 Poems, Riddles, and Songs in 100 Days *and ending with my dad's poems. My hope is that this book of poems will inspire others to challenge and overcome a small part of their dyslexic learning disorder. This book is dedicated to my dad Roy Francis Krueger, my beautiful wife, children, and grandchildren*

About the Poems, Riddles, and Songs

These poems, riddles, and songs were written with the idea to describe certain reflective moments, emotions, experiences, my Christian faith, and different subjects or whatever came to my mind that day.

I didn't study the writing of poetry or elements of poetry. I just went about it with the innocence of writing rhymes. I really wasn't aware of any of the poetic elements or types, feet, meter, Iambic, pentameter, blank verse, free verse, epics, narratives, haiku, pastoral, sonnet, elegies, ode, limerick, lyric, ballads, soliloquy, or villanelle. Surely a lot to uncover and learn about in studying the art of poetry.

I discovered that most of my poems are called monorhyme. In a monorhyme all the lines in a stanza or entire poem end with the same rhyme. I guess if you read all my poems in one day the sounds and the rhymes would sound very similar.

I wanted to convey unpretentious stories, simple, fun, and silly and some with deep complexity. I just let it flow. That's what made it so amusing and fun. It included my opinions, spirituality, and subjects that were humorous to me. Creating some seriousness, laughter, and enjoyment. Most with a rhyming rhythm of words.

Some included riddles for the reader to discover embedded treasures of what I was trying to convey. Here are a few hints, see if you can find them: summer, war, coal, balloons, grandchildren, winter, spring, fall, socks, soap, circus, earplugs, cars, déjà vu, fishing, cookies, cake, moon, sun, stars, imagination, COVID-19,

Christmas, laughter, mouse, common sense, prayer, physical therapist, books, movies, spiritual protection, the Holy Spirit's presence, resurrection, freedom, peace, sports, spiritual battle, dogs, cats, a box, healing, clouds, love at first sight, and many more. Let me know your score.

I can't give them all up so just discover and have some fun.

Blessings,
Jeffrey A Krueger

Note: There are eleven poems that I scribbled out on napkins and sheets of paper prior to September 20, 2021. I thought I would include those in this collection. Most are labeled as rewrites. I rewrote them on the days listed. This collection is comprised of 111 poems.

Autumn Sleep

Colors falling gently one at a time
Quietly mesmerizing my mind

To earth's expression so sublime

Morning fog opens the final door
A last summer breeze which is no more

Fiery furnace blasts orange, yellow, red
Gather off to the graveyard's hedge

Painted blue skies on a canvas sketched
Mirror reflection drawing etched

Shining off the water's edge

Joyful dancing of the color tones
I skip sought-after flat stones

Soon to be under my quilted spread
Curled up for warmth in my bed

Fast asleep it all goes
In a circle before the white blows

In the land of the frosty cold

9/21/21 JK2

Daydream

Sitting by myself
Pulling memories off the bookshelf
Staring down where my feet are placed
On the cobblestone

Sometimes it's nice to be alone

Refreshing to hear silence
In your mind
Remembering
Good times

I think of other folks
Whose lives are a vapor of smoke
Whose lost loved ones
Who spoke

Causing our inner world to choke

Thanking
My great, great grand folks
Who came here
With hope

Continuing the journey
As I approach
A bend in the river
Throw the rope

Hooking the galactic stagecoach

Bumping along
Adventurous road
Reminds me
I'm never alone

At the crossroads
Stand on the mighty stone
Reaching up into the heavenly throne
Believing there's an eternal home

Turning the final page praying all to be saved from a hellish roam

9/22/21 **JK3**

Another Day

*Amazing,
How time moves fast
Reflecting on the past*

*Grow as a child
Through the good, bad, and who can
Being fortunate to maneuver through venomous sand*

*Find a partner that shares
Numbers of the hour and second hand
Standing with you when times are sad and glad*

*Babies, babies,
Your turn to watch and grow
Holding on with all your might to slow*

*From one to three to thirty-three,
Every age we held so tightly
Now given birth to children so brightly*

*Times of tears when our parents go
Retirement comes
Relaxing to sip the Merlot*

*Sharing our aches and pains
Operations allow us to sustain
Minds forgetting where we put things, only to maintain*

*Bones are brittle still dancing to the bluegrass fiddle
Our legacy is not a riddle
Wholeheartedly sacrificial*

Trying to run and play after the little ones
As though it was yesterday
Muscles and endurance start to fade away

At the end of our stay
Thankful for the gift
That gives us time for another day

9/23/21 **JK4**

Politics

Stop chewing gum!
I'm telling you, it's no fun
Unwrapping the wrapper
Isn't for everyone

If you blow a bubble,
You're really in trouble
Causing a pop
Will get your tongue chop

Placing the gum
Where no one can see
Momentarily
Sets us free

Choosing to spit it out
Far to sea
Chewing a new piece
With flavor and integrity

The only way to forge a remedy

Eternity

Last forever, can't you see
There's no end, that can't be

Does it circle onto itself?
What's outside of that continental shelf?

Another horizon of stars and galaxies
Racing by a mind-boggling fantasy

No, it's true, unknown unseen reality
Confuses the mind in its actuality

Guess I'll settle on the round earth I came from
To stop my inquisitive mind from becoming numb

9/25/21 JK6

Deep Inside

Trying to write of things reflected deep inside
Only to discover
I'm searching for something I cannot find

Struggled to describe whispering winds begun
Or rays of the singing sun
Suddenly hearing a gentle voice available to everyone

Listen, listen can you hear?
Soft and silent to your ear
Turning to thunder striking so loud, so near

Running hard and fast
Through connections of your past
Announcing fear, you thought wouldn't last

Filling your cup to the brink
With a poisonous drink
Or silencing that beast to purely think

Tracks have been cleared
Railroad car called fear
No longer scheduled to appear

Peaceful, forgiving voice so sweet
Resting now soulfully upbeat
Reflected deep inside of what I think

Sadness

Trying to sweep it away it's persistent to stay
When my family and friends are so far away

Tragedy, a car accident, a baby's death,
Spouse is gone, we lose our breath

Senseless violence creeps onto the streets
Tears fall down for so many, we weep

The soldier that comes home without a limb
Others who are never seen again

Sex slavery, pornography, how can it be
Sound of the marching enemy

Starving children and death by war
Earthquakes, hurricanes, typhoons, fires, and much, much more

Overdosed young people poisoned on their own accord
Homeless, abandoned, mentally broken, and ignored

What medicine do we take to calm the inner core?
Racism, hatred, abuse, brutality, who is keeping score?

Abortion, open borders, jobs, and pay
Teaching our children, what can I say?

Nation-building foreign conflicts that won't go away
Broken houses gone astray

Divided individuals and marriages have lost their way
Dictatorships, missiles, climate change, power, and greed

Freedoms being torn from the huge oak tree
Red flag is flying for all, can't you see?

Come to grips with our sexual identity
Checking the boxes to reveal our heredity

How do we stop this insurgent of insanity?
Is it the end for humankind's destiny?

No! I saw a rainbow for all today, glistening in the heavenly café
Raining down tickets to the dancing hope ballet

Lassoing sadness from its reign
Blasting open the gates of a peaceful domain

Uncovering the veil of the majestic estate
Colliding with our human fate

Now we pray, it's not too late

Skating

Sharpening the blades before I lace-up
Hot chocolate poured into my cup

Warm long socks pulled up to my knees
Down jacket and hat so I won't freeze

Wool mittens knitted for me
Gives warmth to my fingers so the cold will flee

Steel knives touching frozen lakes of ice
Cutting a groove so straight and precise

Skidding to a sudden stop
Fall to my knees to avoid a drop

Crystal flakes flying everywhere
Revealing cracks like broken glassware

Sliding fast, out of control
Falling into an open hole

Hold my breath, under I go
Looking up at a white piercing glow

Thinking I may have to pack my bedroll
A hand reaches up from where, I do not know

Laying me on my back, wet and cold
Now no longer in control

On that skating day, I know
Love and grace restored my soul

Rewrite 9/28/21 **JK9**

Seated Reflection

Gazing across horizon's space
Emerges a green line
Unseen caresses my face
Stopping time

Click, click captures moments of building trestles
Sand builders dig their holes
Young lads maneuver water vessels
Against the pushing blue cold

Diamonds sparkling interlude
Reflection of midday rays
What voices speak in such solitude?
High above as appendages sway

Playful youth remind the hourglass
Can't stop or pass
A glowing vitality
Finding its path in a childish reality

Who dares command a flowering bud?
Against this silence of tranquility
Which pumps lifeblood
Through our heartfelt serenity

Relish the leisure of this infant field event
Reminded to appreciate the youthful scent
Don't be lost in the pixels of the screen
So not to be entranced into the world of the obscene

Run-Of-The-Mill

Run-of-the-mill, I say
Calling out today

Is it the same when we crawl?
Maybe hard to recall

When grace covers with a shawl
Breaking down the veiled wall

Looking toward the sun
Heat resides and light will come

Lost will not remain
I can begin again

Here to face another day
Reaching each other without delay

I'm leaving, I'm not here to stay

Run-of-the-mill, I say

Rewrite 9/30/21 **JK11**

Graduation

Tiptoes by silently and still
Like waves of water
Seen from a distant steep hill

No longer held in arms of care
Slowly being released
To a world unfair

Rocks laid as tests, unfulfilled
Stepping-stones across
River's chill

Freedom declared
Produces gladness and joy
Young journey we guide like a hotel concierge

Hearts fulfilled
Brings brightness of the sun
Gentle love from everlasting windmill

Always your home a rejoicing bed light
Never alone but shared
Watching the new adventure with delight

Securely prepared

Morning Coffee

A glimpse of time
Hearing a distant chime

Sunrise rays highlights faces
While the maker constructs like a mime

Conversation surrounds steam ascending
From the iron tool

Instructional notes with a voice of direction
Pierces the scent of the tasty fool

Such a delight at this simple sight
After the morning dew

Filling our inside
That tastes so amazing, cordon bleu

Rewrite 10/2/21 **JK13**

Revealed

Through the distant window
Spyglass sees
Hope on the horizon
Isn't just for me

Tap toes
Click heels
Hand of God
Only one that moves to heal

Jumping on the back
Of the pillaging phantom
Striking down the limbs
Of the corrupt stallion

Swinging a mighty blazing sword
Relentlessly succeeds
Meeting the need
Crushing the fearful stampede

Only then
The spirit intercedes
With the likeness
Of a growing mustard seed

Be silent and calm,
The torrent rains
Will cease with a healing balm
When you call on his name

Magnificent Day

In the distant past
Breach in the wall
Reaching to the high mountain
Cushioning the fall

Fiber mesh
Patch the soul
Softens the embedded
Jagged shoals

Journey along
Worn path
Sudden flashback
Memories in my backpack

Fallen stones etch
Many manifest faced masks
Becoming weathered
Into a polished gem clasp

Soaring wings cast
Shadows below
Guiding the spirit
Into a brightly glorious glow

No more searching
For the missing steps
The final breath
Is at rest

Flight takes off
Through the golden rays
Saturated with light
Set ablaze

Returning to the nest
For a comfortable stay
Start again
Another magnificent day

Rewrite 10/3/21 **JK15**

The Table

*Flashing into my eyes,
Like a guided missile,
Through snow-dotted windows
Sparkles like diamond crystals*

*Voices cascade over the table
Escorting a surprised giggle
As a stillness rests
On pines painted
With white drizzle*

*Heat of the inside
Brings forth warmth
From oven-fresh baked pies
Blankets wrapped around henceforth
Providing comfort like the morning sunrise*

*Connecting souls
With an enduring impression
Forged deep in the mortar
That's holding bricks
Of our lasting recollections*

*Engaging
Amusing gifted reflections
Sharing family affections
Resembling a jubilant
Musical jam session*

Rewrite 10/4/21 **JK16**

Family Gathers

Sitting on a swing
Cooling autumn breeze
Caresses my neck

Red oak leaves
Shout out
A blazing respect

Pines nestle together
Waiting
For the upcoming event

The dark blue waves
Move
With an eye of suspect

Young shouts of laughter
Mixed in
With a silent consent

Clinking and clatter
Of servers
Fulfilling appetites suppressed

A family gathers, thanking God for the nest

Rewrite 10/5/21 **JK17**

Terri

*Gazing up into
The magnificent blue sky
Beautiful white clouds
Extremely puffy, passing by*

*Sun shining
Brightly on the golden path
Seeing so clearly
Now grab your hat*

*Time to go
You won't be alone
Waiting for you
To come home*

*For my love for you
Will always be
Deeply embedded
For all to see*

*God's whisper
Of eternal peace and love
Surrounding us
When you're soaring above*

10/6/21 **JK18**

New Life

Hands held tight inside
Reveal the spirits might
Of the young one
Soon to take flight

Waiting for the clock
To strike nine
With a joyous anticipation
Of the newly created design

Wonderful moment
In time
We experience
For our short lifetime

Blue was the surprise
When it was divulged
Long before the forming
Of the bulge

Now two
Will be brothers
As playmates
For each other

Hoping the storms
That may hover
Will be stilled
By the nurturing father and mother

Thankful for above
Being pillars in their lives to unite
Holding onto the blanket of love
That covers them at night

New growing baby
Adding to the family of light
Speak truth, not maybe
In the coming daylight

Giving us fresh eyesight
Of a new life knight
Upon each breath's accent
Preciously, heavenly, sent

10/7/21 **JK19**

Inspiration

As the planet
Changes and grows
Stimulated
To learn what I don't know
Inspirational creative portrait
Of newly painted cargo

Imagination, inventiveness
Candles light
Expressions of genius
Begins to write
Originality on the wings
Taking flight

Ingenuity wrapped in the gift
Of finesse
Comes in the quality
Of expressiveness
Challenge of creativity
Brings out brilliance

Some insight
Wit and flair
Becomes the standard
To dare
A vision and sophistication
That's rare

Rewrite 10/8/21 **JK20**

Poles & Buckets

Whispering sounds
Forest mood
Inner feelings
Joyously being renewed

Quiet moment
Capturing my gaze
Renewing a memory
Catch of the day

Steel tubs approach
Armed with poles and buckets
The running captain helps them remove
They're sought-after lockets

Cool breeze
Warm by the rays
Breaking through with ease
Misty morning haze

Distant sound calls out
Changing my sight
Brassy voices shout
Birds take flight

Where the tan carpets midway
Meets the green
Long walkway
Extends into the blue scene

Carrying passengers
In seated machines
Ready to be predators
Out to the unseen

Rewrite 10/10/21 **JK21**

My Love

Lights reflecting colors of the rainbow's barcode
Causing the heartbeat awoken
Our embrace has spoken
Openly to my heart never to be broken

Because of you
I hear the voice of God tenderly, completely
Whispering of a union, a permanent tattoo
Cherishing a fulfilled life deeply

Sunrises, sunsets, blistering ice storm
Moon sightings stars above
Cold shattered by the warm
Joyful laughter of love

Blending a challenging teardrop
Adventures begin whimsically
Climbing to the mountaintop
Breathe in the spirit anxiously

Moment of tranquility
Embrace with a passionate kiss
Inner splendor of eligibility
Share our time here until it's mist

My arms hold firmly
Union that persists
My love unwaveringly
Without you my life would not exist

Moving In

Seldom I see
Peace clouds reveal to me
Senses observing
Settling in newcomers to be

Silent whispers
Busting buds
Golden dog red
Comes over for hugs

Vast horizon gleaned
Wooden arms stretched out to tease
Patches of blue waves, to be seen
Through a tapestry of green trustees

Inviting summer heat
Breaking winter freeze
Heat of the sun is sweet
Cooled off by a refreshing breeze

Sounds of unpacking
Wedding collections
Precious fool's gold
Treasured possessions

Merging new affections
Of memories keys
Sharing new introspections
Into radiant rubies

Echoes

Traveling passageways
Of my journey when I was young
High water surging
Pouring downward over the falls' tongue

Tears form, past silently awakes
Chambers within
Revealing mistakes
Of deeply scarred skin

Playmate time, no mercy
We turn, take a step
Imbedded controversy
Bittersweet taste, can't forget

Wonderfully peaceful at the cross
Fulfilling a joyful rest
Wounds remain at a painful cost
Consumes sunsets

Enlightening, brilliant rays
Splendor so deep
Uplifting praise
Cradles my sleep

Soul shouts, redeemed life
A newly sharpened knife
Truly worth the embrace
Of forgiveness and grace

Yellow Fellow

Harnessed its powerful atomic mass
Careful piece of class
Magnifies its heat
Distant winter's heartbeat
Laying on the beach
Warmth is so sweet

One million pictures greet
Awaken rises, romantic sets
Fry an egg on the asphalt street
Win some bets
Joy pops out to meet
Your sight on a dreary day

Moving closer, amazing rays
Melts ice away
Dance in the heated spray
Be careful when it's all-day
World of eyes sneak a gaze
As its neighbor covers its blaze

Mystical voice of rainbows awakes
Glistening diamonds off snowflakes
Prisms of light
Reflections off the lake so bright
Friendly when we're lost
Showing the way in the sky's exhaust

Some call it the indicator of the soul
Created for our existence, heat control
Symbol of divine power
By only one high tower
Colors scattered by the atmosphere
Only yellow, orange, red, in the troposphere

Beach Boys, Stevie Wonder, Beatles
Wrote its splendor in song
Pine Ridge Boys one of the first rising eagles
To play along
Time to say good night, it's gone
Working so hard all-day

Hoping you never go away
Seeing you rise another day

Lost and Found

Impressions
We hope will last
Of recollections of the past
Stored information on the flag
Of sailing vessels jiggermast

Where is my phone
Can you call me?
Can't find my keys
Lost my glasses, I can't see
Where is my car, thought I parked in aisle three?

Age can stunt the echo
It's lost
In a mindless meadow
Keeping visual pieces
Of the art deco

Precious commodity
Stored in the organ
Documenting your odyssey
Short term, long term,
Amnesia, a mystery

Jubilation when
Sharing with others
Humiliation when you forget
Names of your brothers
Dementia affects more mothers

Clear tangles in form of tau avoided sepsis
Extract the amyloid
Disrupts communication of the synapses
To cells deployed
Slowing the disease by certain steroids

Oh, how I cherish
My trusted companion
Pray I won't lose my way
Standing at the edge of the canyon
Thankful my neurons reside in an uncluttered mansion

The Present

It's my size so tall and wide, wonder what's inside
Rip, rip, rip, tear, tear, tear
Scraps of ribbon and paper flying everywhere
Starry eyes wide with excitement
Uncovering a new treasure of enlightenment
Peek inside to see my prize
Two large ears, what a surprise
Shake and shake, but it's not alive

Shouts out loud!
"Hold it up so we can see"
Confused look from the gallery
Is it a fox or some socks?
Robotic arm with batteries?
Could it be a house for a mouse?
Or a car with accessories
Throwing it up and out so I can crawl about

No, no, no, don't push it aside!!!!
That was expensive and hard to find
But I like my house,
My car with accessories,
All the things it could be
Grab my crayons and pencils
Scissors and glue, change it into
Something new

Doorway or window or a cage, like at the zoo
Where my long new trunk can stand on a stool
Or can stay while I'm at school
Lay my head on its fluffy, silky, fat belly
Dreaming of tomorrow's breakfast of toast and jelly
Closing crayon painted shutters to the kitchen deli
Pull up covers of the warming wool
Falling asleep to the moon so full

10/16/21 **JK27**

Trust

What's lurking behind the door
I thought I knew
But I don't anymore

Took all the life preservers off the boat
When it's sinking
It's not a joke

Many people are fooled joining the scam
Beware, cement is cracking
On the face of the dam

A lie is the truth, the truth is a lie
I am so confused
It's making me cry

So many commentators, opinions with a spin
Doctors, professors, entertainers
Looking like the same mannequins

Media networks, newspapers, politicians have they sold honesty?
Or are they all fooled in acting out
The enemy's perversity?

When I wake up, will daylight be night?
Will justice draw its sword or abandon the fight?
Or will the shadows prevail, extinguishing the light?

Can we build a new land of confidence and hope?
A firm belief
Of what Martin Luther King spoke?

Are we condemned to be victims of the past?
Will we continue
To treat others as outcasts?

Who called us to surrender our fleshly stronghold?
I AM, the only one
Who can break the hateful mold

To shatter the impenetrable cold
Bringing us back alongside kindness in love
A supernatural strength from high up above

10/17/21 **JK28**

Happy

A new puppy and kitty for all
Receiving a graduation diploma, stand tall
Ring the bell defeated the cancer wall

Newborn baby
Barbecue picnic with the whole family
Inhaling first summer breeze from the balcony

Soldiers come home
Winning the Super Bowl in the dome
World Series, you're not alone

First date and car, now you're free
New home on the lake, we agree
Hole in one, it shows up on the marquee

Taking money out before the stock market crash
Meet your soulmate, a wedding bash
Finally growing a Fu Manchu Stache

Skiing down the first powder on the slope
Breaking addiction, now you have hope
Heart is strong listening to the doc's stethoscope

Grandchildren speak the darndest things
First live gig and I didn't break a string
Met the famous drummer who wore a lot of rings

Got the job I studied for so hard
Finally processed my green card
Becoming an American citizen, I joined the National Guard

They found me a home, so, so sweet
Me and my children are off the street
Receiving food, thankfully not numbers on a spreadsheet

Billions of actions make us feel this way
Causing a million treasured heartbeats to sway
Maybe you can add some more to the happiness sleigh

Bully

Stop pushing
You're cruel and insulting
Arrogant and threatening
Aggressive and menacing
You pick on the weak
Seeking out the meek
Try someone your own size
Do you have hate inside?
Leave them alone
You could break their bones
Have you heard this on the phone?
Hurting people hurt people like a kidney stone
Punching and hitting
Could you try knitting?
When will it end?
Do you need a caring friend?
We're praying that you can be saved
Don't be lured away to the burning grave
You have a knife and a club
A gun to show off to the gang at the pub!
You shot someone, you're to blame
It's the end of the game
We tried to help
You just kicked us away
Now it's a long prison stay

Time to think of what you lost
Harsh reality of what consequences cost
We won't give up on your life
Hoping divine intervention saves your soul for the afterlife
Second and third chances are his powerful grace
His redeeming power is now for you to embrace

10/19/21 **JK30**

A Sign

Falling from grace
How can it be
Why sinful and ordinary me?
Given a sign of healing and hope for all to see

Freshly born again with God at the helm
Peering into the heavenly realm
Blinding white in the distance
Shines brightly for an instant

Removing the drought
Love reaches out
Flowing all around
Double rainbow touching the ground

Listen, a quiet still voice
Reflecting on the turquoise sea
Amazing grace to believe
A divine message shown for me

Embracing the decree
Of the speaking word of the MC
Lifts me up, sets me free
To mobilize a new divine legacy

Spirits' presence gives cleansing soap
From the anointing oil of the olive tree
A sign of healing and hope
For all to see

At First Sight

I was frozen
Like headlights shined into the eyes of a deer
Tripped over my feet
Getting unnoticeably near

Beautiful image
Overwhelmed my mind
Everything stopped
In a twinkling of time

Asked for a dance
Got swirled around
Captivating scent
I couldn't calm down

Voice like a butter knife
Spreading joy, ending strife
Angel speaking
Harmonious sounds I've been seeking

Radiant, enchanting eyes scan
Pulling me closer to hold my hand
Looking deep into my soul
Hormones leaping out of control

Arms around my neck, a soft whisper
Nodded my head as a slow drifter
Do you want a kiss?
Yes, I'd be foolish to miss

Flesh meeting, my eyes closed seemingly
Emotional fireworks stimulating my inner being
Instantly became lost in a rainbow of electricity
Confirming first love has authenticity

Knowing at this moment this was from above
My soulmate forever, my beloved
Precious gift of one's happiness
At first sight and a kiss

Fluffy White

Incredible shapes
Slowly moving into my air space
Can you see an alligator or an elephant?
A funny face?

It's so peaceful
When they cover pieces of the blue
Wonder what it would be like
To ride on one too

They can gather quickly
Turning black as coal
Dumping inches of rain
Or heavy snow

Summer heat a hot bandit
Atmospheric blanket
Cools down the surface
Helping protect the ones that concern us

Tiny water droplets and ice crystals
Mixture of both, currently wispy cirrus missiles
Puffy cumulus, tall nimbostratus, and stratus
High above it just passed us

When they touch the ground
Calling it a fog
It's a lot different
From the city's smog

Filled with a sense of wonder
When gazing at this beauty slumber
Initiates such a relaxing moment
Of the creator's miracle components

Incredible puzzle pieces in flight
Waiting to get my gaze back into the fluffy white
Imagining another horse leaping
In nature's paintings of shaped greetings

Rewrite song Heart notes 10/22/21 **JK33**

Divorced Child

I've got no responsibilities
I've got none at all
Got no mommy and daddy
Got no love at all

I am a divorced child in the land of the free
Hey, hey, yeah

Living on city streets
That's what feeds me to stay alive
Keeping in the beat
Can't hide my love inside

I am a divorced child in the land of the free
Hey, hey, yeah

Can't get enough thrills
By taking all the pills
You asked me why
I got so high

I'm a divorced child in the land of the free
Hey, hey, yeah

De de divorce child
De de divorce child
De de divorce child
De de divorce child
De de divorce child

Rewrite song Heart notes 10/23/21 **JK34**

Keep On Smiling

*Woooooo
Every day of my life*

*I'm telling you
You don't have to frown
Cause there's love all around*

*Every day of my life I can see it
I'm telling you
So, believe it*

*Can you see the birds up in the sky?
You don't have to look very high
To see them flyyyyyyyyyyyyyy*

*We live for peace
So, take my hand
Like the living things
Throughout this land*

*Every day of my life
I can see it
I'm telling you
So, believe it*

*Keep on smiling, smiling
Keep on smiling, smiling
Keep on smiling, smiling
Keep on smiling, smiling
Keep on smiling, you don't have to be sad*

*See the smiling faces all around
See the smiling faces all around
See the smiling faces all around*

I'm telling you
You don't have to frown
Cause there's love all around

If you can make it through another day
If you do
I can stay till tomorrowwwww

Every day of my life, I can see it
I'm telling you
So, believe it

Keep on smiling, smiling
Keep on smiling, smiling
Keep on smiling, smiling
Keep on smiling, smiling
Keep on smiling, smiling

Everydayyyyyyyyyyyy

Risen

Let me tell you about a time
When it was all about the crime

Found myself standing on a curb
Intoxicated by the herb

Waiting for the sign
To change my mind

Being struck by the intoxication
Of the blind

Like a blanket falling from the sky
Tried to hide, making up an alibi

Body became acidified, liquefied
Vision transformed like a butterfly

Thought I was going to die
Became oversupplied, identified

Like a spike through my hand
Felt banished from this land

Hourglass filling with sand
That moment was preplanned

No more secondhand
Crossing into meadowland

Reprimand to understand
No more contraband

Time to unload my pride
I crossed the line, it was nullified

Completely finalized

Rewrite 10/25/21 **JK36**

#2

He was six, could catch a football
Got sick at school
His sister came to his class walked him down the hall
Sliding down the hill, Soo Pass ranch he ruled

New home and a bedroom
Watched over his new sibling buddies
Played Mario downstairs in the family room
Rather than do his studies

Stayed with his dad for a while
Loyalty, he had was real
Travels back with a smile
Love couldn't be concealed

Tricked his friend with near beer
Basketball, football, baseball the winner
Many parties when we weren't near
Swimming in the pool before dinner

Send him and his sister home on a plane
Drama I can't explain
Vacation in Cayman
Stayed in and watched OJ

Snowmobiles, jet skis, almost a killer
Eighth grade dated a pretty blondie
Hockey wasn't his pillar
Hunting, fishing was his cup of tea

College was a little silly
His main class was golf, got an A
Maintenance with Larry listening to Willie
Eighth-grade sweetheart became his marriage bouquet

First baby a shocker
What a wonderful joy
Another in the hopper
One more a boy

Move three times before the farm
Divided that was a heartbreak
Stumble into our arms
Redeemed and killed the snake

Master builder was his fate
Sales exec, make no mistake
Worship music, open the gate
Grown man of means wants to live on the lake

My first son I ever knew
Some called me a step that made me sad
Adventure with nickel pickle that was grand
His soft heart, I love that lad

Bow Wow

When they arrive, they are so cuddly and beautiful
Watch your shoes, they may become unusable

New teeth as sharp as a razor blade
Toilet paper shredded, he ate my hearing aid!

Oh, he's just a baby, don't paddle his behind
Take him to the doctor, his stomach is in a bind

Look how he has grown, leaping, jumping, he won't leave you alone
Throw it until your arm is sore, never stop retrieving that bone

Pet on the head, a stomach scratched
Ears laid down ready to lay beside you, were heavenly matched

Come running when it's feeding time
When they escaped from the yard, you're left behind

Alert you when the squirrels and chipmunks run by
With a sniffing nose, they can tell when someone's high

Licking my face, a washing they don't hesitate
Steal a cookie right out of my hand, into your kennel, close the gate

Protects the children, he shows his teeth
From any alien intruders they know they can beat

Speak to them in a language they understand
Somewhere between a baby's dribble and a captain's command

Most loyal companion, it's hard to say goodbye
Part of the family, I'm not going to cry

My best friend, the most precious loss, I can't deny
Love and affection you can't buy

10/27/28 **JK38**

Friends

Mysterious, magical, magnificent
Sometimes very innocent
The bond is the test of an everlasting powerful scent
Never ambivalent

Who hooks the anchor to the ocean floor?
Keeping the waves from taking the oars
When adding up the dos and don'ts
At the end, there's no score

Molten gold poured into the mold
Inserting jewels around the crown, connects what's true
Holding up our soul
When we fall to the submitting fool

Reaching out through the haze
Giving us comfort when stuck in the maze
Agreeing to disagree to nullify our drawer
Filled of relied on opinionated dossiers

We embrace our souls
With a passion of vulnerability
Not to be confused from the masks
Of our own stupidity

Standing to fight with might
With an uncompromising zeal
To allow the vine and the branches
Intertwining as strong as steel

Breaking down the walls
Of offenses and petty bitterness
We struggle on the road
Of total forgiveness

Never forgetting the help given
Through our sickness
Rejoicing in the unconditional love
We share as our witness

Angel's Touch

Pull, press, and stretch with pressure till it's met
Is it angels' hands, I bet

Strong and stern with precision
Going deep, deep, deep to heal the incision

Oh, oh that hurts, too much pressure
Needs to be released, let's measure

Feels so much better
Turnover on your side, pull up your sweater

Stories and laughter sometimes sleepy eyes
Oh, that feels good, are you surprised?

Healing hands, a magnificent gift
Revolving door, no one gets missed

Sit up now and catch your bearings
So you don't stumble looking for Red Herrings

Check the schedule my friend
Hopefully you're healed so you won't have to come again

Alive

Swaying brown sticks with painted green tips
Revealing the door to mini spaceships

Opening wide all the glass frames
Renewing the freshness of the outdoor games

Air playfully flows over the pointer
Moving fast along our way, we join her

Busting buds start waving like flags
Thousands of wing dragons emerge playing tag

Harden cement has gone out turning blue
Jumping in the air a splash, sounding like a kazoo

Blankets pulled off little heads start to peek through
Yellow, blue, and red copied for many tattoos

Warmth shatters the cool
Starts the flow of the green pigment of renewal

Puffed-up gray opens, drops hit the floor
Splash, splash, splash, as it starts to pour

Sounds of things chattering and moving about
Peering through the newly formed web as it scouts

Coats are removed as we crawl from our shelters
Hundred shades of one color, captured by a timelaps projector

Take time to see because it's fast fleeing
Heat of the sun changes all from sleeping

11/3/22 **JK41**

A Face

Come quickly at last
Darkness cast
Look
Crystals glisten off the brook

Blood pressure drops during
Wolf howls
I feel a stirring
Like the eyes of the owl

Looking up its indisputable
When looking back
Exquisitely beautiful
Fully clothed in pitch black

With my soulmate
Romance can't escape
Magnetic pulls trait
Affecting the landscape

Pleasure, pain, joy, and sorrow
Ingredients in astrologers' bread
Always my friend to borrow
Guiding me to the water's edge

Mostly white but orange embrace
When I go to bed
Always a comforting face
Staring down I hear a voice, let's pretend

Celestial observance to attend

11/4/21 **JK42**

The Choice

Scratch, scratch, scratch *leaping up to eat a bat*
Acceleration reaches sixty miles flat
Mighty roar five miles away blows off your hat

Jaws that can crack open a tortoise shell
My striped fingerprint is never the same, you can't tell
Leap fifty feet or more, it's time to say farewell

Having my tea and crumpets up in a tree
Careful, it might eat thee
Preferring a size only up to my knee

Those little folks get intoxicated by the nip
Circling around, falling down, it's a trip
Fast and furious to get a mouse, in their grip

Rub against your leg to get a pet
These little creatures don't like to get wet
Loyal companions don't stray far from home, they don't forget

All kinds of colors, a litter of eight
Pick the little runt, don't make a mistake
Soft and cuddly they'll keep you awake

Let me be clear about what you choose
The one with the mane will not only eat your shoes
Seven other kinds will claw your head off when you snooze

A word of wisdom, stay with the domestic breed
They'll snuggle to listen to your heart; they won't make you bleed
Having two, Hurley and Luna, I did concede

11/5/21 **JK43**

Whatever/Seriously

Trying hard to limit my cursing
Oh, what the heck you effing idiot
Understanding the allotment of mercy

Calling for service they tell you 8:30
Your morning activities starting with this recipient
No phone call, no update, they show up at 10:30

You dial the call you crash into a phone tree
They say this technology saves time, thirty minutes, no affiliate
Yikes, disconnected what's behind this curtain we can't see

There are two cashiers for two hundred when there should be thirty-three
Require fifteen minutes early at the doc's, mask on, the word pops up, asphyxiate
One hour later, It's hard to believe

Ordering two brand new warranty batteries
Delivery shows up thirty days late
Only one battery and it's a different variety

Hard to hold back the anxiety
Friendly skies are breaking down with no reasonable update
Cancel flights with no complacency

Trying to get a new phone anxiously
Can't understand the service rep, it's hard to communicate
My conversation is being sent into some far-off fantasy

New grocery list for the thief of the one-world society
Forgive me for my swearing tongue, I know it's just the bait
I'm so thankful for my sobriety

Looking forward to the heavenly dynasty
Humble patience has to be my fate
Holding back the charging anger, giving me clemency

No expectations accepting no vacancy, graciously
Ending the insurgents of the fleshly irritated snake
So, I reverentially wait patiently

11/6/21 **JK44**

Simple Pleasure

Kicked back in the lounge chair
Viewing the latest on a seventy-five-inch hardware
So much streaming, it's electronic warfare
Episode after episode it's become a love affair

Black and white started with brothers Lumiere
Color, thirty-five mm, seventy mm, now digital you can see the fibers in the hair
Editing, diffusion, animation, aperture, computer-generated, don't stare
Comedy, horror, romance, adventure, action, science fiction, I declare

Editing scenes of a documentary, narrative of recorded images
Outdoor theaters are all about gone, now it's called vintage
Spectacular sports coverage not reflecting the real-life scrimmage
Drifting into a pleasurable world enjoying virtual stimulus

Large, buttered popcorn, candy, pop, the big screen, grandkids along
Two hours of excitement it's surely worth fifty dollars to tagalong
Many moons ago it was thirty-five cents, that's ancient history forever gone
Millions of costs, production, special effects, actors' fees, and to feed Kong

Viewing in 3-D hurt my eyes, but it was a thrilling surprise
In the comics who is the strongest superhero that can't die
Something Wars, Lord of the s'more, Potter who can fly
So many great adventures, West Side, Hur, Rose, a list saved, it made me cry

Fighter who ran up the steps, a guy went back in time
Wizard behind the curtain meets Poppins, Alexander is stomping a rhyme
Austria sound, fiddler is frozen, king with a mane, dirty is dancing on a dime
Goes on forever, you might even meet green, mean slime

It's a marathon that lasts all-day
Bring your snacks, sleeping bags, you can all stay
Pick from hundreds or what's happening today
Maybe a docufiction or a real-life depiction of Broadway

Feels so good, transported in time, what a thrill
Exciting, stimulating, cozied up and comfortable, I need a refill
Viewing for hours is extremely cherished, not like exercising on the treadmill
Laid back in the lounge chair, a pleasurable moment of time to chill

Origination

Extending my experiences and thoughts
Into a handcrafted dimensional NFT basket I bought
Throwing it through a portal, it got lost

Edison, Wright Brothers, Ford, formed a lot
Zuckerberg, Bezos, Musk, a new plot
New visions about a flying yacht

Concepts, external objects, not present in my mind
Novel narrative, I conjured up three patents defined
An invention, creation, a solving problem design

Construct hypothetical future scenarios that may or may not exist
Capture that line from a book for an assist
Like a telepathic chromonic calendar on my wrist

Einstein said it will take you everywhere
I must agree with that affair
When blasting off into space in my armchair

Don't turn off the faucet when they say your heads' in the clouds
You may be the next Carl Sagan of your town
Maybe Disney who started with a mouse that ran around

Guardians Spear

Golden falling tears
Coating the guardian's spear
Stop! I command you, dimly lit reflection in the mirror

Oh, please let me come in, I'm so near
I will slay you in battle, you shadow of fear
Crushing the stronghold of your grinding gears

Listen, listen young folk
Don't carry that yolk
Release the haunting blackness from its cloak

Climb to the top of the watchtower
Claim your destiny this hour
Reaching out for your cleansing inner power

Allowing the smoke and debris to clear
Opening the canals to hear
Launching the boat from the pier

Softly through the water it goes
Sails catching the wind unopposed
Joyous symphony composed

Who now stands against the guardian's flock?
Trying to turn back the hands of the clock
Walls have been broken opening the lock

Trying on your new glasses, it's not for style
Walking on the road of a new lifestyle
Shattering all the hidden backup files

Sun shines brightly anew
Giving strength to make it through
It's all temporary, except for you

Rewrite 11/9/21 **JK47**

#1

Marriage to three
Ready-made family
Sitting beside me as I play the guitar
She was eight, had some scars

Heart-felt spirit closed inside
The blooming artist she couldn't hide
Five-foot-three, a basketball star
High school fight, driving a car

Brother, she took care of
New brother and sister she cherished
A gift from above
With open arms she nourished

Crash jet skis, she went too far
Lived in the cabin for a stent
Yellow short hair, a little bizarre
Dog named Tember with no scent

Little green truck perfect fit
College graduation who knows where she went
Stumbled in the black valley's armpit
Redemption and freedom, no more torment

The boy who was just a friend
Scooped her up, marriage ahead
Two beautiful children, million-dollar dividend
Apartment, art studio, then homestead

Beautiful communicator with the divine
Apple pie, Morny's kind
Horse and donkey weren't left behind
Mowing the ranch, a heavenly find

Farm animals, vegetable garden, making bread
Her mother and sister as best friends
My first beautiful daughter, a golden thread
I love so much, truly a godsend

11/9/21 **JK48**

It Conquers All

Comfort the newborn, the hungry, and the lost
Nurturing my children with no score so soft

Humbling myself to serve others
Hugging my loving mother

Protecting as a father
Polite and civil to my sisters and brothers

Loyalty amongst friends
Persevering to the end

Gentleness and embrace
Passionate kiss for my beautiful mate

Excepting each new day with hope
Gentle words I spoke

Calm with trust around the bend
Patience and truth as my friends

Seeking justice kindness for all to see
With commitment and honesty

Modestly clothed to honor completely
Releasing faith, joy, and peace for eternity

Popped

It's bouncing upward, out of control
Blue, green, and red

Don't poke a hole

Rub it on your head instead
Makes your hair standup

Let's pretend

Draw faces on it becoming a wobbly friend
Tap it back-and-forth

Don't let it hit the floor!

But I can't blow it up anymore
Pop! A startled stare

My blue friend is gone, it's not fair
I won't be bored or have despair

Because green and red have settled on the baby's highchair

Oh, Hold Me Tight

Forgive me for my wrongs
Can't seem to fit in and get along
Death and carnage I still see
Hoping the kids won't blame me

Oh, hold me tight
Oh, hold me tight
Oh, hold me tight
Please don't leave tonight

The Purple Heart didn't heal the wounds
Scars and trauma surround like a typhoon
Fear and terror embedded in dreams
Holding hands, your soft whisper, I so desperately need

Oh, hold me tight
Oh, hold me tight
Oh, hold me tight
Please don't leave me tonight

I was strong and tough now I'm a broken man
Each morning I can hardly stand
I can't lose my heartbeat
You are my bright light, walking stick, keep me from saloon street

Oh, hold me tight
Oh, hold me tight
Oh, hold me tight
Please don't leave me tonight

I'm not leaving you, only on death do we part
You're my precious love, I will help us get a new start
I'll wash you, feed you, and read stories of our past
You are my shining knight, a gift from God and it's going to last

I will hold you tight
I will hold you tight
I will hold you tight
I won't leave you tonight

11/11/21 **JK51**

I CAN SEE

*Vision
Of the razor's edge
Slow-moving freight cars
Seen above the hedge*

*Messages written
Along the rattler train
Predicting a warning
Of the coming rain*

*Hold the candle closer
So, I can see below the flame
Images of a chessboard
Reveals a checkmate, ending the game*

*A world with cracks
Volcanoes spewing black
Some read the tea leaves
Revealing the time of the attack*

*It's all written down
In the book
Deliberations spelled out
Sometimes overlooked*

*It's not hard
To decipher
The encrypted code is revealed
By the piper*

*Dreams, predictions,
Words and provisions
Hold tight
For storming angel's insurrection*

Allowing you to see
Through the iron meshed wall
As it crumbles down
Receiving all

A sighting
From a far-off land
Seeing so many buried in the sand
I now kneel before the great I Am

11/11/21 **JK52**

Precious Gifts

Come look for me
Tug and pull grab some chalk
Careful of my sore knee
Plastic pieces that interlock
Wooden squares built so high
Knocked down what a surprise
Race car track, kinetic sand
Snuggle in my lap with blankie in hand
Toy soldiers, ninja turtles scattered about
Let's watch a movie, let's not shout
Can I have a snack
Steal your nose and I won't give it back
After picnic lunchtime
You need to nap
So, I don't have a heart attack
I want my mommy boohoo
Wipe the tears
The fanny too
Who taught you that word?
I'm not sure I heard
I'm scared I want to go home
Can I call my daddy's phone?
That's a funny frown
I'll tickle you, you crazy clown
Dolls with skirts and kitchen plates
Are we having tea or is it too late?
Getting cars open the gate
Now I'm done
Play the drum
Jammies, socks, and underwear
Grab your knapsacks from over there
Where's my stuffed animal
My little bear
One more dance

Around the table, you prance
Now I'm totally out of energy
Come settle down you little fleas
Oh, time is up look who's here
They'll take you home, my little dears
Give me kisses and hugs
I can't wait for the next time, you little bugs

Timeless

Some can play it by ear
Harmony of the lyrics
Draws us near
Moving powerfully through the atmosphere

Universal language for all to understand
Scores and composition heard clearly on a grand
Keys and notes opened on the stand
Played by breath and guided hands

Intoxicated by the soulful mood
Orchestrated so I can barely move
My heart beating a prelude
To the rhythm of the groove

Transported to a world onto its own
Such gratifying tones
I don't feel alone
Covered by a blanket of dancing hormones

Skillful reflection transposed into emotion
Captured by a time capsule explosion
Endless melodies
Of joyful memories awoken

Unity, continuity, vibrations, dancing in celebration
Instruments singing cheerful interpretations
Joining in an exhilarating conversation
Harmonic frequencies surging through the nation

The rate of speed, the tempo
Considered basically fundamental
Unleashing the message
Outwardly transcendental

Passionate voices
Of the inspirational choir
Composed to set your soul on fire
Now recorded in the timeless halls of the versifier

Shadows Conquered

Don't trust the shadow
Behind the man
Beware of the magician's
Sleight of hand
Shell game has been planned

Cast light on the umbra
Where you can't see
Hold tight to the honor of your legacy
They will try to slander your name
Because you believe

Flaming arrows try to hit you from all sides
Hold tight to your mighty shield
As you yield to the bride
Deny the applause of the crowd's appeal
Holding up the banner of pride

Interpret the ancient scrolls
Many will come as learned schoolers
So, you won't be alone
Present rulers
Will be dethroned

Their castles, gold, and jewels
Will have no meaning
It will all disappear
While they're sleeping
Running into the streets screaming

Draw your sword
With your helmet on
Lead the charge
For those who belong
Protective presence keeping you strong

Don't look upon all that's burning
Keep your belt tight, breastplate placed
When you're returning
Lace your boots high
Trouncing scorching lava with eyes discerning

Came under my shadow from above
Enter my kingdom of peace and love
Joining joyous parties
As I gather up all the armies
Detached from the destroyed land

Forever separated by my hand

French Word

I feel like I wrote this
Before
Like repeating a
Beethoven musical score

It's a strange feeling
Little light-headed reeling
Like seeing another world for a minute
I don't regret it

An act I've already done
A person I've already seen
Intuitive experience begun
A mystical dream

Instantly stops my thinking
Slow-motion awakening
Pondering the curiosity blinking
Of a memory that's escaping

Unique voice calling inside
Certainly, an inquisitive surprise
Sectors of my mind that hide
Hard to describe this prize

Passing quickly on a magical hike
Resembling opening a drawer
I feel like
I wrote this before

Snapped

Crawling along the outdoor garden hose
Trying to find a warm place
Before the winter wind blows
Oh, I see a little hole

Can I squeeze into that little crack?
I'll stretch out like a rubber band
On my back
Falling into a hanging backpack

Oh, it's warm and cozy in here
I smell something
Very near
Running quickly, the coast is clear

It's brown, soft, and tasty I think
One step on lightly, do I hear a klink?
I'll eat some more
Then move on for a drink

Metal bar comes crashing down
With a snap!
Oh, I think it broke my back
Eek honey! remove the gray critter from the trap

Throw it outside the window glass
On the hardened brown grass
It's still alive it hasn't passed
I'll crawl away not moving very fast

Never going back to that crack, safe at last

11/15/21 **JK57**

Day by Day

Sun slowly peeks through the window
Raise my head bringing my mind back from limbo

Open the curtains to see outside
Relieve myself, wake my bride

She throws back the covers
Maneuvering the others

Dogs and cats crying aloud
Morning news tales of disaster, a dark cloud

Visiting with our father
Devotions and prayer we try not to be bothered

Breakfast, a shower, social media, a game
Check our mail, voice messaging, it's all the same

Young ones appear
Lunchtime switching gears

Physical therapy workout and swim
Large latte no flavor, hot to the brim

Early evening now it's dinner time
News again, truth to find

Then the wheel, a movie treat
More news, it's bittersweet

Brush our teeth, head for bed
Medication to ease the aching head

Kiss and hug, snuggle up under the warm blankets
Dark night brings toss, turns, a dream of a banquet

Sun slowly peeks through the window
Raise my head bringing my mind back from limbo

11/16/21 **JK58**

A Child's Wound

Come close my little friend
Pull them down once again

Place your hands behind your back
Or I'll give you a mighty slap

It feels so good doesn't it, don't lie
Help, help, help, from deep inside

I need to run but I can't hide
He's so strong I can't move, I tried

Innocence broken as I cry to heaven
Who can I tell, I'm only seven?

Okay, we're finished here
If you tell anyone, I'll hurt you my dear

Pleasure spirit is it a sin
Arousal keeps coming, I can't win

Oh, how long will I be harassed?
Internal trauma will it pass?

I've seen your tears behind your mask
Bringing healing to your wounds just as you have asked

Breaking that stronghold, the enemy cast
It's broken now the scars are in the past

Oh, thank you, Lord, for that at last

11/16/21 **JK59**

The Harvest

*Start at three, some at five, or seven
Skates, clubs, balls, bats, footballs, helmets, sticks, gloves, bags, and nets
Might be eleven
We say it builds character, strength, and leadership
Working together as a team strengthening relationships*

*Run, pass, kick, skate, catch the ball
Don't make a mistake
Working on who's the best we can make
Sifting through the ones who are lost
You made the team, do you measure up, at what cost?*

*Your life is dedicated to this dream
Only to find out
It's unbearably extreme
Parents push, shove, scream at the refs from up above
Supposed to be fun and exciting, but not for some*

*Moves so fast
Through the age
Don't think about scars it made
College coaches now for some
Selective harvest has begun*

*Schools and coaches
Receiving mountains of gold
TV deals made, who cares about the athlete's soul
Building billion-dollar stadiums like coliseums of old
Draft for a selected few, the rest are left in the cold*

*Section of TV news dedicated to this cultural stew
No payments due
I'd like my business each night
To be on the news
No fee, I couldn't lose*

Owners and players making millions
Being glorified as heroes too
Voicing concerns to help society, do they have a clue
I love sports, I'm like you
Pull back the curtain, have we been fooled?

Ace, racers pace, home run ruled
Faster engine tooled
One putt, a Hail Mary, slap shot, fastball, jump ball
Punch in the face, or slam down on the mat, a brawl
Ref made a bad call

Money, money, money, is that what it's about?
What a haul, it's got a lot of clout
Entertainment pleasures turn to angry frustration
Meanwhile, are we secretly losing our nation?
Caught up with our pleasure, we just change the station

A Delight

Crunchy and chewy dissolves in my mouth
When it's hard I dunk in coffee or milk
Hoping it won't go south
Take off the cover
Lick off the cream

Get a sugar rush
Sometimes too extreme
Sugar, flour, butter, and eggs
Mixed in the bowl to refrigerate
Flatten, pressed, rolled, with textures freshly homemade
I can't escape

Straight out of the oven
A dozen or so placed on a large plate
Aroma is incredible
They're too hot, I can't wait
Served up for any occasion I suppose
Christmas holds a lot of weight

Sprinkled, frosted, cut into shapes
Cream filling, ready to bake
Don't get confused
It's not the HTTP text files to consume
Alfajores, Bizcochito's, Hamantaschen, Rugelach, Pfeffernusse
A delightful smell in the room

Peppermint, cinnamon, vanilla, maple, butterscotch
Strong perfume
So many to pick from
Where to start
Thick, thin, six-inch or small, crisp, flat, fat, plain, buttery, sugary
A shape of a heart

Some fancy, same are the same
Sweetly delicious at the end of the buffet
Now there's a large tray I'll try to savor
Don't want to get a stomachache
Count all the flavors
Don't leave one out and make a mistake

Peanut butter, chocolate chip, oatmeal raisin
Snickerdoodle, windmill, lemon, cornflake
Pizzelles, red velvet, macaroon, biscotti, sugar,
Gingerbread, pecan, brown sugar, pumpkin
Apple, brownies, bars, fudge-covered, crinkle, meringue, spritz, shortbread
I'm dunkin'

Oh, I think I forgot one
King of all
Little, round, circle, cream-filled zero
Stack so tall
Oh yes that scrumptious black hero
In one sitting you eat them all

11/18/21 **JK61**

Ring the Bell

Priceless, fragile, a commodity so needed in the rivers of humanities landscape
Speaking of emancipation, a sacred treasure that we must believe to succeed
In our conscience of openness and goodness of our liberties are they being secretly erased?

Seeing from the mountaintop unrestrained characteristics how they have been shaped
A confidence of seeking opportunity and the self-termination of our rights
What sword pretends to slash at our indulgence of our sovereignty, in the darkness of night

Is the door closing on our serenity and tranquility of our known independence?
Are we struggling to lose our autonomy as it's slowly being suspended?
Constitution the diagnostic tool so discreetly states our mandate

Written by spirit-filled men it conveys the following edict without restraint
Rights to religion, speech, press, assembly, petition, and twenty-six more
We the people determine the quality of life without hindrance or neglect, don't close the door

Can the Statue of Liberty still sing?
Do we need to add to her sculpted form some wings?
We are privileged to have freedom of choice not to be imprisoned or enslaved

Called out loudly for grace and kindness to surround our human rights, now let's be brave
Swim through the waters of freedom of choice, to continue the fight
For our civil liberties with all our might

Hear the distinctive voice of solidarity
Do not abandon justice or the pursuit of our happiness, sign by thirty-nine of thee
We have the privilege and responsibility to carry the torch with clarity

Our saving grace can't seem to come from our own humanity
Oh why, oh why can't you see this coming tragedy
Visions with a discerning eye see a new roadmap of topography

There's another script we need to review
Written for both me and you
There lie the deep truths to be consumed

You may not believe that the angels will ring the bell
But surely you can smell
The stench rising up from Hell

Drop to my knees to hear from the power above
The war for freedom isn't against flesh and blood
The enemies' insurgents will be struck down by the dove

In the end, all will win, who come behind the ultimate force of love

Countless Treasures

I'm transported
Into another land
Love the feel
Of this in my hand
Thinking I'll travel to
A warm place with sand

Today a cowboy, tomorrow an alien
Resembling a disfigured man
Many pieces and places
Available on the stand
Volumes upon volumes
Of things I don't understand

Giving pleasure and comfort
Nestled in front of the fireplace
Codex from ancient scrolls illuminating
Stories about the human race
Amazing pictures
Catapulted me into outer space

The epigraph
I can hardly read
Paging through the document
That resembles graffiti
Giving me insight and understanding
To its meaning

Now I'm on the shores
Of an ancient city
Tomorrow I'll be in a gunfight
Which isn't pretty
Traveling anywhere, teaching, instruction, illusion
It's so whimsical and witty

Some use it to
Hit you over the head
Or stack it up to stand on
To reach the ledge
Prefer to cradle it
In my bed

Romance, intrigue, with helpers
When in need
Thrillers, chillers
Suspense indeed
Truths and hope
Mixed with some religious history

Precious treasure to relax and captivate your soul
A gift of a simple pleasure
Like winning the game by a field goal
Flying, running, or walking for miles
Or just take a stroll

Sandwiched between
Two covers
Waiting for you
To discover
Pages and chapters
Of a universe for you to uncover

11/19/21 **JK63**

MDD

Hard to see when the room is so dimly lit
Fog circles around, it won't quit
Walking on a tightrope wobbling within

Can't get out of bed, sad emotions surround my head
Feeling exhausted I'm not sure I can get fed
Headaches, joint pain, cramps, discomfort, how long will it last?

Nourishing on hopelessness instead
Withdrawal into hibernation, hiding under my bed
Sleepless nights insomnia, a stigma I dread

Discouragement and despair as I sit in my armchair
Someone turn on the light, I wasn't aware
Feeling nothing at all, despondency, dejection, a cold stare

Will I ever get out of this maze? I'm so scared
Flamethrower burning anxiety into my flesh
Confusion set ablaze, this I can't express

I'm lost, can't find my way through this desolate mess
Medication, therapy, it's becoming too complex
Melancholy, misery, gloom escaping this hideous room's address

Calling out for help to breakdown this impenetrable wall
Seems like no one hears me at all
Silence creeps in spinning loneliness like a gushing waterfall

That's not the number I called in tears
Reconnecting to a new voice I've been longing to hear
Flashing through black swampy goo coming near

Releasing the vicious cycle that captures my brain's descend
Saving grace has broken in revealing my divine friend
Allowing me to live and love again

11/19/21 **JK64**

Meal for Two

Sailing through the air hitting with a splash
Lower it down without a crash
The plastic piece stays up floating, will it last?

Patience, patience, patience
Quit knocking around only the stillness will draw them near
Checking the screen, I think they're over here

Bobber went down, that was fast
Set it tight, I think you got one at last
Don't let up, oh wow, it snapped

Patience, patience, patience
Let the line out again don't cast
Reel it in slowly not hard or fast

Sun is just coming up
Perfect time to pour some coffee in your cup
Morning breeze feels so good a freshly pickup

Patience, patience, patience
I'll start the motor and move over here
Maybe drop the anchor, no I think I'll leave it in gear

Worms, minnows, leeches, take your pick
Hook them right or they will have a picnic
Your rod is bending, keep it up, that's the trick

Patience, patience, patience
Reel it in don't let up, or it will take you for a ride
Bring it close to the port side

Grabbing the net, I'm right behind
Oh wow, it's huge! No wonder it broke the line
It's got to be forty pounds or more, oh, so fine

Patience, patience, patience
Color is beautiful, what a thrill!
Lifted it up, I'll grab it behind the gills

It will flop and buck so hold it down on the bottom
I'm not sure it'll fit in the live well, but you caught 'em
Slimy, scaley, slippery, smelly, absolutely gorgeous

You got the catch of the day, and it was enormous

The Little Tree

Family gone, a lonely Christmas Eve
Home alone, no ornaments, no lights, no tree

As I sat by myself in my grandma's house, something spoke to me
Christmas spirit I believe

Left the house and walk down the block
Drawn to the very last tree on the lot

Four-foot-tall, thin and sparse unsought
Needed a home on that eve, not to be forgot

Salesman said you can have that, little boy
Hopefully it will bring you some joy

Dragged it home over twelve blocks
Up to Granny's attic to find dusty ornaments and lights in a box

Stood it up and placed it in the stand
Little tree's voice sang out majestic and grand

Not a balsam, spruce, Douglas fir, or Norway, but a Scotch pine
Placed the angel on the top, a candy cane hung with some twine

Emptied the box, pinecones, icicles, red balls, and frayed string of lights
Two bubbled ornaments yellow and blue, yet very bright

What was left a lighted cross, I hung in window, good news
Spirit of the moment chased away the blues

Sat back in the tattered living room chair
My ninety-three-year-old German-speaking grandma came in and stared

She sat down next to me and started to sing the latter
"O Tannenbaum o Tannenbaum wie treu sind deine Blätter"

The cross began to cast a brilliant red light
Little green was illuminated almost supernaturally bright

As I sat and stared my soul begin to fill with joy and gladness
That little tree chosen that day, taking away the loneliness and sadness

The Hunt

Set up the cameras six months before
September through January, I hope I score
Several big bucks
I see even more

My palace is nestled high above
Scouting and preparation, it's all done
Fifty-pound compound, carbon arrows
My true love

Wait and wait, between three-thirty and five
Out several days as weeks go by
See him on the cam portrayed
Same time each day

Easton gold tips, colored pins, one hundred feet away
Get a glimpse I draw my bow, he won't stay
Heart is pumping my breath withdrew
Still like a statue

Coming back another time to get you
Sun goes down I'm on the ground, I won't forget to
Jump in my four-wheeler, I'll be back again
Next time you'll be the fool

Perfect condition no wind at my back
Cool November, slight snow, I see his tracks
Now he comes near, only fifty feet
It's time to attack

Adrenaline is pumping, draw the bow slowly
Perfect broadside shot aiming behind the shoulder, confidently
Release aid in hand, I gently squeeze letting the arrow fly
Boldly

Looks up for a moment then falls to the ground
Record buck with horns all around
Latex gloves, sharp knife, precise cuts to field dress
Help hold him down it's a hunter's process

Off to the butcher, I must confess it's released the stress
Venison steaks, ground burger, sausage, and the rest
Sticks and jerky into a freezer chest
Another great hunt to feed the nest

Oh Daddy, Oh Daddy

Oh daddy, oh daddy
Will you not stay out all night?
Please come home so there won't be a fight

Oh daddy, oh daddy
Quit shouting those horrible words
She's screaming back in no uncertain terms

Oh daddy, oh daddy
Let's help you into bed
Looks as though you've cut your head

Oh daddy, oh daddy
What happened to your job?
You lost another one, it makes me sob

Oh daddy, oh daddy
You spent what little money we had
How are we to feed ourselves, this makes me so sad

Oh daddy oh daddy
Just want to hold you tight
Don't want to be scared tonight

Oh daddy, oh daddy
They've called again
Have to get you, this has got to end

Oh daddy, oh daddy
I can remember a few hugs
Now you're sick and they're killing your pain with drugs

Oh daddy, oh daddy
You can no longer speak
Lost your throat and half a lung you're so weak

Oh daddy, oh daddy
We had so little time
I'm going to finish your book you started of rhymes

Oh daddy, oh daddy
Praying I will be with you
Paddling the Celestial River together in a canoe

Contagious

I couldn't stop
Its breaking down
My mental blocks
Hilarity
Like an electrical shock

Giggling uncontrollably
My stomach got knots
Smile is stuck wide
Like a fifty-foot yacht
Can't catch my breath
My lungs might pop

Gleeful parade of clowns
Dancing on the boardwalk dock
Makes me chuckle inwardly
When wearing their striped purple socks
Mood is struck into irrepressible symphony
That rocks

A positive tittering
Howling with joy
Reading of one hundred jokes
All in one ploy
I'm slapping the table
Wildly, ships ahoy

I can't help it
I've peed my pants
It struck the funny bone
How long will it last?
Amused with happiness
Remembering comical times in our past

So much fun and ecstasy
Infectious medicine we need
Keeps us healthy
From the negative bleed
I snicker
Then a guffawing decree

Filled with gaiety
Warm and tender to the heart
Except in the movie theater
When someone seeps
Smell of a dead carp
That may sound crude, but that's where it starts

I'm cracking up completely out of control
Can't suppress the reaction
What happened in the show
I let it go
That movie episode captured my childlike silliness
Exhilarating my dancing soul to playful dizziness

Song 11/23/21 **JK69**

I Want to Know

I want to know, I want to know soooooo
Is it time to find out, love divine

I want to know, I want to know soooooo
Ring me up, don't let me down, spin me around

I want to know, I want to know soooooo
Has love gone cold that poured out from our souls?

I made my bed where I lay my crown
Reaching for my pen leaving a note to express a smile not a frown

It's my world inside my head, connecting the living and honoring the dead
Circus of fools who lost their tools I sadly dread

I want to know, I want to know soooooo
Why should I cry when I gaze up into the beautiful blue sky?

I want to know, I want to know soooooo
Traveling the mountain's path reveals inspiring secrets to my past

I want to know, I want to know soooooo
Hearing the voice of love penetrating my heart from above

Who knows the answers to this riddle I found?
Of a counterfeit master trying to enslave my love in this compound

You can ask all the questions as you go around and around
Stepping off the merry-go-round, I discovered my heritage that created me from the ground

I want to know, I want to know soooooo
Now I know faith, forgiveness, grace, and love is my dancing show I found

Song 11/23/21 **JK70**

Christ the Jesus Emmanuel

Christ the Jesus Emmanuel his birth proclaimed
Over the hills rejoice hallelujah, hallelujah, shout again

The night sky lit with stars of angels of love
Rejoicing and shouting the Saviors come

Christ the Jesus Emmanuel his birth proclaimed
Over the hills rejoice hallelujah, hallelujah, shout again

The hope of peace cast down from above
Filling our hearts with love for everyone

Christ the Jesus Emmanuel his birth proclaimed
Over the hills rejoice hallelujah, hallelujah, shout again

Dance and celebrate for our souls are changed
Giving gifts of compassion and kindness to all the same

Christ the Jesus Emmanuel his birth proclaimed
Over the hills rejoice hallelujah, hallelujah, shout again

Everlasting light to show our path
A glorious eternity that will come to pass

Christ the Jesus Emmanuel his birth proclaimed
Over the hills rejoice hallelujah, hallelujah, shout again

The savior's grace received as living water from the well
On our knees giving praise casting out forever the darkness of hell

Christ the Jesus Emmanuel his birth proclaimed
Over the hills rejoice hallelujah, hallelujah, shout again

Justified Nonsense

Breaking glass revealing the wetlands
Sun colored with crayons by little hands
Spiraling downward caught by the circus band

Who's causing the plants to grow?
Ouch, I stub my toe
Can't believe choking weeds start the show

Riding on a pony, turn the storybook page
Hastily moving props to an unknown backstage
A king's found the ransom paid

Misery packaged in doubt homemade
Drawing from the shadowy fountains poison sea
Shaded glasses so a blind man can see

Strike the match set ablaze
Hanging upside down in a cage
Dry grass ignited, a glow in the haze

Fool falls down the hill
Somersaults break the spell
Of a strangling chain that kills

There is no reason, sometimes no rhyme
Digging deep to capture the treasure of time
Is this the season to be kind?

Peanut butter sandwich maybe bologna too
Joyfully laughing, now I conclude
Justified nonsense, hiding in the glue

11/24/21 **JK72**

So Precious

Got a call they said it won't be long
Come to a clinic to escort her along
When I got there, they said she was gone

Go to the hospital instead
Am I late as I poked in my head?
On went a mask and a gown, they pushed me ahead

Looking down as they cut
Getting dizzy, I had to sit down on my rump
A gentle voice turned her head, "You'll be alright, my buttercup"

Sounds of slushing, swishing, and suction, bouncing off the walls
Doc said, "Come look, he's got balls!"
Standing up I took the first glimpse, eyes closed so perfect and small

Peering in the glasshouse, he raised his hand in a wave
First connection deep down, it will always stay
God's perfect gift to celebrate that day

My little buddy, I couldn't stay away
Helped me paint, fix, and play
Ninja turtles and weapons marching in an array

A star in commercials to sell tickets
Brought him on stage for all to witness
Decked out in a cowboy hat and boots, little Mr. Slickness

Sister has come his way
Both climbing ladders, placing ornaments on Christmas day
Instructing the orchestra to play

Baseball, football, hockey, soccer, basketball he did his best
Didn't matter to me if he won the quest
I knew deep down it was his mind that would win the test

Throwing him in the air in the swimming pool
Diving off the raft, it was so cool
Riding on my snowmobile and driving a car, was I being a fool

High school, college graduation, an engineer, how time flew
European trip, that was a jewel
Marriage, a move, it seems so far away

New little buddy has come, hooray
With a brother who's made his way
I'm not leaving, I'm going to join this parade

11/25/21 **JK73**

A Joyous Manuscript

Colors falling on the ground
Leaving all the sparsely sticks brown
Sleepiness has gathered around

Frigid wind circling through the town
Last chilly rain, laying down a slippery gown
Skidding sideways creating a meltdown

Ohhh the first white, so beautifully bright
Crystals appearing reflected by the light
Cuddle around the fireplace looking out at an amazing sight

Cover up, it goes deep to the bone
One layer, two layers, three layers, you won't smell the cologne
Gloves, boots, mittens, and hats, a jacket you have outgrown

Footprints you can follow
Angels engraved in the soft hollow
Silent peacefulness, you can hear yourself swallow

Thick and solid you can drill a hole
Let down your line from your pole
Stoke up the little wood stove with charcoal

Whizzing down the hill
Amazing fluffy powder test your skills
Black diamond moguls, do you have the will

Gripping the motorized apparatus with a colorful helmet of fashion
Speeds you can hardly imagine
Traveling miles and miles with an exuberant passion

Sun goes down minus, minus, minus, with a mysterious shyness
Time for a moonwalk that disappears the busyness to unite this
The only sound heard: a crunching of snow and wind beside us

Hunker down, fifty-mile-an-hour blowing fiercely
Drift ten feet high, it touches the sky nearly
Hardly open the door, barely

Morning sun appears, golden rays revealing an astounding, pearl coat
Frosted branches dripping with glistening gems like seeing through a kaleidoscope
Seasons of wonder revealed through a celestial telescope

Joyous manuscript written in white, expressing the cycle of life fashionably spoke

Second-Go-Around

Think we need to go
Into the car speedily off to another show
Checked in, you have a special glow
IV hooked up, you're only at three
You need to walk around the hall, wait and see
Twelve hours later it's time to let it be

Behind the screen
Smarter this time, not looking down on that cutting routine
Oh, Doc you need some help to intervene
Stood up with a nervous concern
Blue and purple, I feel my stomach churn
Cut, cut, cut, the cord around the neck, the breath returned

Open the airway with a suction syringe
Eyes open completely, no reason to cringe
It's all okay, the purple and blue changed to a pink-full grin
So tiny with larger eyes completely opened and bright
Surpasses the light of the stars and the sunlight
Jumping up and down crazy with the delight

Riding on my shoulders the mode of transportation
Reading stories drawing on the back each night with affirmation
Destroying the ninja turtle set-up with an abandoned celebration
Brother, she mimicked with love and admiration
Short hair tomboy named Kevin
Fishing pro by the time she was seven

Playing in the sandbox, driving a pink motorized car, then a bike free of holding
Swimming on the bucking bronco's back, it may be called jolting
Piano, trumpet, guitar lessons, a sweet spirit filled unfolding
Florida fantasy land, a houseboat adventure
Birthday parties celebrated as a joint venture
Driving lessons, maneuvering around fifty-gallon barrels like a superhero avenger

How could it be a prom dress, snowball queen, time so fleeting
Beautiful, absolutely gorgeously speaking
Playing hockey, I started shrieking
Soccer, basketball, she played so hard, high school and college graduation
Apartment with a dog in the backyard for protection
Marriage to a pirate she so loved, a beautiful selection

Two children, amazingly perfect when I looked through the nursery window
New home on the lake like finding a rare pink flamingo
My precious baby forever, never to be in limbo
Mother, wife, daughter, and aunt, I had to let go
Beautiful memories I will always dearly hold
Lassie Lou, Lou Lou who I never had to scold

She's truly a precious princess worth more than a million bricks of gold

Riddle of One

If you don't wash them, they'll turn rotten
Flannel, nylon, wool, bamboo, polyester, and cotton
For every birthday I got some

Where did that hole come from, a snag?
Eek stinky, funky, right out of the gym bag
Hold my breath, I'm going to gag

Knitted garment for the lower part
Giving warmth and comfortability a woven art
Sometimes decorated with tiny little hearts

A pad, stop rubbing, absorbing, cushioning, moisture control
It's a lot of things this pair must know
Friction and blisters, it must go

Ringworm, fungus, bacteria, it can all grow
Need these friends to stop that show
Simple gift helps those who have a season of snow

Puppies chew on them
Compression ones pressed tightly to succumb
Doc says wear them, don't be dumb

Why is there only one do you suppose?
Got eaten by the other clothes?
Or did it just decompose?

Can you discover the riddle of the one that covers your toes?

11/28/21 **JK76**

My Favorite

Green is in full bloom
Hundreds of shades of a multicolored costume
Fully awake the warm breeze to resume
Bluest color of the rivers and lakes
Singing and shouting, come in we're awake
Grills cleaned up to cook some thick steaks

Fishing line cast off the dock
Dip your feet in the water, take off your socks
Paddleboard, kayak, canoe, the gentle waves rock
Asphalt is hot, don't burn your feet
Morning golf, the temperature is rising, oil up with sunscreen grease
Motorboat, tubing, slalom skiing, let the rope release

Jumping on the lilypad, diving backward off the raft
Air mattress, snorkels, and goggles underwater at last
Mowing and trimming the luscious green grass
Squirt gun fights, I pull out the hose
Coughing and gagging, water up the nose
Sand toys, inner tubes, baseball, whiffle ball, bocce ball, I'm close

Swatting monster mosquitoes as we gathered around the fire pit
Ten thousand stars in the night sky, brightly lit
Roasting marshmallows, they're burned a bit
Stories and laughter, I don't want it to quit
Festival music we can hear as we sit
Having a few, I must admit

Flowers blooming and bees consuming
Leaving the city, pack up the RV, were leaving
Pitch the tent by the falls, fresh air now I can stop sneezing
Maybe we will encounter a big black bear
Chickens and rabbits seem agitated, should we be scared?
Thankful for the small county fair

Cows, pigs, goats, and horses, those are the things we like to share
Tractor pull, the demolition derby, a lot of black smoke in the air
Birds singing, squirrels running, chipmunks chattering, it's all so sweet
Vegetable gardens, alfalfa, soybeans, corn, and wheat
Beaver, muskrats swim close by, eagles soaring, what an amazing feat
Sitting on the deck sipping the morning coffee with raised feet

Taking a bike ride around the freshwater, the great escape
Home fireworks show we ignite, don't make a mistake
It's so hot I can't get out of the lake
Pull out the dock, raft, weed roller now, the cool is coming it's getting late
I could mention another one hundred things but it's all passing, that's what I hate
Revolving door to the next season now I can't wait, for our next suns hot date

11/29/21 **JK77**

High Above

Warm-blooded, my flying friend
Feathers, toothless, try eating again
Broke out of an egg I see your little head
Sea, flight, and water all outdoors
Theropod dinosaurs

Reptiles from avialans
Visual signals, calls, and songs
Flocking and mobbing, they'll knock off your hat
Live in terrestrial habitat
Pets and food feeders never-ending

Racing, message sending
Religious symbols
Wisdom they speak in hymnals
Coats of arms in a visual decree
Soaring, elliptical, high speed
Eighteen thousand species, a balance of nature's power

Fastest 186 miles an hour
Largest twenty-six pounds
Little ones flying backward like tiny clowns
As high as thirty-seven thousand feet
Bald king is so sweet

Watching them soar
So high up above
Some will land on you if you have a leather glove
The beauty of such incredible creatures
Is learning our surroundings by these amazing teachers

Breaking Free

Not me, I won't let you see my mood swings

Why are you so late?
Did you forget the time and date?

Had to stop and get some things

Are you okay?
Should we meet another day?

Hello, hello, are you there, ring, ring, ring

I have some pain I'm nauseated
I'm irritable and frustrated

You seem scared and overwhelmed by some invisible imposter

My compulsion and paranoia are coming out
The demons are swirling all about

I see a vision, the craving that's feeding the habit, a ghostly monster

It had me chained down for years I've been enslaved
The compulsion is deeply engraved

You're so weak, time to be discovered, you're standing at the gallows

I'm shaking violently with tremors
Self-destruction is at the center

Stop watering the ground of the dark shadows

Can't dodge them anymore
I need to escape but I'm caught in the revolving door

You're sweating and shaking sickly, you need healing, not another dose

I'm fixated on driving a nail through my hand
Poison's horrible but the pleasure is grand

Wake up, you've overdosed, save your life that you tried to dispose

Release me from the cement cast that has me entombed
Before my body and mind are totally consumed

I pray a supernatural strike to penetrate through the rancid clothes

I raise my head to see a blinding light ahead
Risen from being almost dead

I'm glad the wrecking ball has set you free, no need to foreclose

Spirit has filled me up, I don't question the sovereign power
Thankful for my second chance, to climb to the top of the watchtower

12/1/21 **JK79**

A New

I let it go for so long

Can't prolong

Finally get a chair

Getting a funny glare

How do you want this to show?

Cut it up, shape it up, let's go

Relaxing buzzing sound

Snip, snip, snip, it hits the ground

Lay my head back for a rinse

Massage my crown, I feel like a prince

Hot towel and shaved a minor nick

No apologies, it was really thick

Brushed off apron aside

Now, brown bear, you're cleaned up, go outside

Tip the man and jump in my car

Radio blasting, feeling like a rockstar

12/2/21 **JK80**

Spongy

There're many uses

Concerts, football games, even church too

Disappearing easily, did they fall in the stew

Some red, yellow, some are blue

Loud bang in the canal hall

Stop by the cushioned wall

Twisted into shape, pushed in so small

Keep a dozen or so they seem to fall away

Small plastic container to keep them from going astray

Absolutely needed when I try to rest at noon

After school kids come running in, it's too soon

Remove my little friends because I need to participate

Soon it will be evening, I can make another date

Lay my head on my pillow for silence to begin

Little friends are back, I'm falling asleep again

Morning as the sun arrives

Lift my head two fell out I can't find

Now they're back for the silent time

12/3/21 **JK81**

Choice

Thinking helmet of the fool

Launch in the underground school

No longer makes freedom tools

Melted woven colors thriving

Stalling the tapestry of the magic carpets driving

Harvest breath that's reviving

Look around, you barking hounds

Don't slip into the abyss and drown

Army of conspirators won't back down

Escape from the deteriorating city

Enter the kingdom of pillars of pretty

Protected from the world's self-pity

12/4/21 **JK82**

The Designer

Colorful wallpaper pasted up on the wall
Laying of bricks up so tall
Beautiful chandelier hung on the ceiling
Hand-carved door open, revealing
8,981-foot bridge across the bay
3.3 million cubic yards of concrete holding water back, I pray
Rocket ships blasted into space
Satellites, computers, lasers, curing diseases, it's a race
Heart transplant, robotic prosthetic arms, and legs
Automated chicken farms producing millions of eggs
Where there's a design, there's a designer's many pegs
Billion neurons to help the light processing of the retina
60,000 miles of blood vessels, eight round trips from the US to Calcutta
600 muscles covered by the tent that regenerates itself
37.2 trillion cells, thinking, speaking, and feeling, 130 million on the bookshelf
8.7 million species, 50 billion birds, 3 trillion fish, 10 quintillion insects
That's not the complete list, I checked
If the sun was placed one million miles closer or farther, we would be toast
Having an atmosphere that protects us, I must boast
You don't have to look hard to see it revealed
Cocoon turns into a beautiful butterflies' wings
Tadpole transforms into a frog that sings
I really must ponder
When I'm thinking in the wild blue yonder
Where there's a design, there's a designer

12/5/21 **JK83**

Our Home

Can't see all of it, I understand
Sometimes only where I stand
Outer station reveal is grand

Titanic plates that migrate
Third neighbor to congregate
Two caps of white, too cold for a blind date

Woven blanket called the hydrosphere
Been around for almost four billion years
Inner and outer cores creating a magnetic sphere

Seeing from the flying bird
Beauty you can't describe by words
Colors of the rainbow your heart is stirred

Mighty house with biodiversity that abounds
Butterflies to elephants that stomp around
Many rooms occupied even underground

Diamonds, rubies, coal, now lithium a digger's prey
Molten rock pouring into the bay
Structures upon structures the green is in the way

Needed breath that's so profound
From every corner a warning of desperate sound
Creation in the universe where no other is found

Intellect from one species seen
After the paintings will the brushes be cleaned?
Will all be lost falling into the desolate ravine

Colossal winds of power and destruction
Huge amounts of liquid covering construction
Changing landscape is under reconstruction

Then the essence of all will be washed away
A new multi-color ball emerges to stay
Cosmic rebirth that will be part of that day

Two Left Feet

Sing, whistle, hop, and stomp
All around
So much fun to bebop
Turn up the sound

Swinging, tapping, ballerina
Refreshing sea breeze
Lifted off the grounds arena
Flying in the air with ease

Partners or choreographed
With friends
Swirling in a downdraft
Don't let it end

Drumbeat and bass
Filling in the space
Whirled around, sliding in place
To my knees with Grace

Foxtrot, polka, waltz, swing around
Don't let me go
Jitterbug then free-falling down
To the rock and roll show

Macarena, rockettes, tango
Spinning like a top, it's happening again
Last allemande an aerobic Rambo
Grab my hands, trust me, join in

12/6/21 **JK85**

WAR

Cain and Abel might have encouraged the first
Conflict Megiddo runs into Chedorlaomer's thirst
Beginnings of the generational curse

Clubs then maces, catapults, swords, and spears
Axes, daggers, chakra, shuriken, gladiators feared
Battering rams, arrows, flail, morning stars appeared

Rifles, machine guns, artillery, meet me on the dance floor
Hand grenades, bazookas, tanks, ships offshore
Napalm, missiles, nuclear hydrogen, tsar, who's keeping score

Drone, radar, laser, infrared, ADAPTIV camouflage
Supersonic, OMFV, XM25, IVAS, it's a barrage
T Ghost, Taser Shockwave, MAHEM, nice entourage

Aristocracy, colonialism, communism
Democracy, Marxism, socialism, capitalism
Monarchy, theocracy, dictatorship, Nazism

Propaganda, diplomacy, terrorist, some intel
Mercenaries insurgents, revolution ring the bell
Militias, freedom, danger of control, a road to Hell

Power, control, strife, danger, greed, revenge
Kings, emperors, czars, fascists, back to Stonehenge
Conflict, suffering, famine, invasion to avenge

Blast, explosions, shrapnel, suffocation, burns
Mutilation, broken bones, amputation, no returns
Obliteration, annihilation, genocide, no concern

Hoping to change the matrix printer
Can we stop the trigger finger
Or will Armageddon be the final stinger

Frosting

You say it's your birthday, one candle or two?

Chocolate, white, or vanilla filled, all for the crew

Swirls, flowers, crisscross, lavender, and blue

One layer, two or three, a wedding tier so high you can't see

Delicious with ice cream poured on honey from the bee

Raspberries, blueberries, strawberries, it's great with coffee or tea

Grease the pan, flour, eggs, and sugar, will it stand?

Bake in the oven made by scratch, by hand

Scrumptious aroma lifted in the air, so grand

Lettering and scenes of all kinds portrayed

Sometimes large sheets made for a crusade

Everyone should get one on their special day, I pray

12/8/21 **JK87**

Deep in the Hole

Theophrastus 371–287 BC to see
1571 Sir Bruce of Carnock Scotland quay

Deep dark hole of the colliery
Underground start at the pit head

Gaseous poisons better chance at the lottery
Collapse of the timbers can make a deathbed

Steel wire light, the hidden flame
Stay away from the firedamp gas

There's no time to blame
Cribbing works, will the roof last?

Fusion fan, a must needed tool
Fresh air intake, that passageway, don't block

Jack-leg used is no fool
Refuge hole, move aside, don't get dropped

Human casualties can be a lot
Fifty countries use this mineral, can they stop?

Anthracite, bituminous, lignite we got
Burn safe is a scientific hopscotch

Today we burn it because that's our lot
Future discoveries we may need not

Save the soul from the burning lung
Soon to move on, can we use the sun?

Mining this resource has never been great
Honoring so many who gave their lives for us, we thank

The Gathering

Fourteen chairs gathered there
Around the living room circle
Intended hearts of raised up prayer
Like scented incense in the tabernacle

Songs of praise, powerful worship fervently
Expressing joy of the coming birthday
Heard a chorus of angels singing in harmony
Creating a joyful harmonic wave

Silent Night opened the door into the soul
Igniting a bright light
Such a tenderness and peaceful goal
Of the Holy Spirit's might

Not just a natural emotion growing
Supernatural expression began
Tears flowing a connection of all-knowing
Of a sweetness at hand

Away in a Manger continued ensemble
With silent cries inside starting to flow
Simple boombox of musicians assemble
Creating a musical presence that glowed

Hard to convey in words the expression heard
That moment of knowing the baby's quest
Completely bathed in the living word
Of salvation giving us a hope of eternal rest

Time stopped as God wrapped his arms around us
Saying what a child is this
Completely consumed by a divine love bus
A gathering I'm glad I didn't miss

12/10/21 **JK89**

The Embrace

Returning home from active duty
Surprise!
Children greeting at end of the workday
Don't hide

Running to grandpa and grandma
Give us more time
Walk in the door at Thanksgiving
We blow our mind

Lifelong friendships
Say goodbye
Family Christmas so many greetings
Not a dry eye

Warm blanket of fleece
Wrapped around
Tears flowing as the pressure is increased
Almost a knockdown

Momma and papa so inclined
A child's lifeline
So, so sweet
Don't let go, it's complete

Thank the nurses
At your release
Firefighters and police
For the rescuers' peace

Graduation party
So many, I'm sore
Feelings so hearty
We passionately adore

Arms around a squeeze session
Pat on the back
What happens if the greatest expression
Of love got hijacked

12/11/21 **JK90**

Blue, Blue, Gray, Gray, White, White, Black

*Blue, blue, gray, gray, white, white, black
Many stacked on top of a truck's back*

*Gray, gray, white, white, black, black, blue
Classic, premium, standard, pinstripes are cool*

*White, black, white, black, gray, gray, red
Steam, gas, electric, perpetual motion ahead*

*Red, blue, blue, white, white, red, yellow
Passing by, you might see a handsome fellow*

*White, white, black, black, blue, gray, gray
Why so many dull and drab colors today*

*Gray, gray, gray, white, black, black, green
Bloodhound 1000 MPH you wouldn't be seen*

*Black, gray, gray, green, red, white, white
I'm going to paint mine frightfully bright*

*Yellow, white, white, red, blue, blue, purple
Maybe they'll add rainbow rubber circles*

12/12/21 **JK91**

May the Light Be with You

Mountain boulders crashing down
Found myself spinning around
Which way should I go?
Not sure I know
East or west, I seem so lost
Should I try the deep valley, at what cost?
That's the adventure I should do
Even though I don't have a clue
A challenge I need to make
Even if I make a mistake
Never tried, win or lose
All in, that's what I choose
Can't predict the future
I won't be a moocher
Living life without a risk I might miss
Could be lost or dismissed
Searching to find
My destiny to help mankind

12/13/21 **JK92**

Coming to Town

It may have started by Maximus in Rome
Philip Astley began at Ha'penny Hatch, others then later in a dome

Parade of colorful wagons came down the road
Erect the big top it's time to unload

Colorful striping of yellow, blue, white, and red
All hands-on deck to complete the massive spread

Just watching the setup was a delight for all
Open the gate, watch your head, don't fall

Three rings of red, yellow, and blue
Dancers, jugglers, and magicians, it's fun to be fooled

Balloons, hats, cotton candy, and popcorn, get ready for the show
Tiny stagecoach full of clowns with suitcases of cargo

One-by-one they keep coming out, a constant flow
How do they fit in there, I don't know?

Ringmaster shouts with his top hat displayed
Introducing the unicyclists crisscrossing in an array

Lion tamer snapping his whip at big cats in the cage
Putting their arms on his shoulder, jumping up on a small stage

Lights are dim, the spotlight is focused in
Look up at the swinging trapeze, no net to catch them when they spin

Hush from the crowd as three somersaults begin
Flying through the air caught by their hands, roaring applause and grins

Tightrope walker flinches, we become all nervous, the line is so thin
Drum roll starts, spotlight lights up, balance seems off, will we notify next of kin?

His helmet placed on; he waves as his body is loaded into the cannon
Mighty blast shakes the big top, he sails through the air caught by the net companion

Screams and shrieks, standing clapping hysterically in joyful bliss
Parade of elephants hooked tail by tail, riding on top, the monkey's kiss

Horses prancing, exquisite costume women riders sliding down on the Arabians' side
Band of acrobats tumbling, flipping onto each other's backs with pride

Dogs of all sizes jumping through fiery hoops
Cleanup-clown shovels up the poop

Packed up at night with a positive decree
Travel to the next town to bring joy and happiness for all to see

12/14/21 **JK93**

Fucanglong

Skin of iron scales tattooed deep crimson
Bathing in the resinous darken pool
Scorched black barbs on the tail sharpened
By the rocky tools

Blasting a flaming breath
In the myrtle misty hollow
Now my throat is burning
Blistering raw, it's hard to swallow

Descending into the blackened dungeon cave
Thine conquered landscape
Slithering along, the gold never touching
My wings-stretched cape

Resting here I wait
For the next foolish fellows
Who test my patience to motivate
Cremating souls succumbing to the furnace bellows

Swing fifty feet one way dusting east
Hidden wealth of king's bouquet
Sulfurous bubbling gas released
Keeping lava golems in my stairway

Raspy voice of enchanted tones discharged
Keys that open the gate
Who trespasses into the cavernous horn
Flashing swords as bait

Lured by the treasures, I see
Standing in the river, come closer to me
Fiery blast melting intruders' skin to vapors of steam
Liquefying bones into a distant, whispering scream

Approaching army marching around
My welcoming next prey
Soaring high above the volcano crashing down
Crushing them to pieces of clay

Settling down on treasures of gold, silver, and diamond wonders
Of the many royals
Sworn duty as the guardian protecting from treasure hunters
Including the powerful pearl

12/15/21 **JK94**

Citadel Homecoming

Blueprints drawn precise, exact
Crane, chisel, saw, time to extract

Cut into frozen blue
Blocks of magical translucent hue

Stacked high almost touches the sky
Courtyard, throne, sculpture, dragonfly

Playground of lights, joy for everyone
Captured memories of winter fun

Children, grandchildren gather around
Witness the moment, placing the crown

Music enhancing, colors dancing
Warm fires, it's enchanting

Wonderful time under a blanket of cold
The slight wind blows flakes of amber gold

Hats, mittens, boots, coats to keep warm
Playing in a mystic, charming art form

Polar jamboree, an exhilarating plunge
Rejoice King Isbit, homecoming has begun

12/16/21 **JK95**

Preparing

Rushing, mailing, buying, wrapping
Music playing Jingle Bells, foot-tapping

Tree chopping ornaments popping
Lights hanging, place the wreath, continue shopping

Plan the menu, Italian or ham
Ask the kids what they would plan

Ten days left, it's out of hand
Baking cookies, I can hardly stand

Picking names out of a hat
No more than twenty dollars, and that's a fact

Head to church, early service out of three
Light the candle, Silent Night, a tear to set you free

Knock at the door, greetings to all twenty-three
Placing presents under the tree

Hold hands for prayer, finish the dinner, stuffed to the top
Kids waiting to open presents, you can't stop

Choose a Santa to hand out the gifts to share
Rip, rip, tear, tear, paper and ribbons everywhere

Out to the fire pit to burn colorful wrappings and boxes too
Celebrating the birth with family, that's so cool

Remembering to stop to make the choice that rules
Rejoicing with God who sent Jesus to save us, the once-lost fools

12/17/21 **JK96**

Wounded

Deepest root of grief
Unbearable to keep

Run down in a parade, for dancing it cost her
By an out-of-control steel monster

How do we handle this grief?
Lives taken like a fallen leaf

Another school shaken
Young gunman now forsaken

Despair the neighbor of grief
The enemy is working hard to destroy our belief

Candle factory destroyed
Devastation to the second shift employed

Hundreds of calamities before, overcome by sadness and grief
Who is keeping score of the anguish, sorrow, the companion's thief?

Heartache and suffering are too much to take
Prayers of faith for the shattered souls tormented, causing a quake

Labor pains of contraction, tragedies causing uncontrollable tears in grief
How do we calm the waves of so many lost, crashing on the reef?

Over our lifetime the essence of lives will be lost
Will we ever receive peace and comfort, at what cost?

Shock, disbelief, denial, guilt, anger, depression, the bundle of grief
Healing and gaining our lives back, will there be any relief?

Scars masking the wounds never having full recovery
Hoping for a reunion in the heavenly's of a rediscovery

A must needed, supernatural, seismic encounter to walk alongside our grief
Giving us courage to believe someday we'll meet

For our continued journey here to be complete

12/17/21 **JK97**

The Week Before

'Twas the week before Christmas
Home from New York, I think the animals missed us

Should have picked a tree before we left, it was a test
Got to pick from ten Charlie Brown's, second-best

Scurrying to decorate the house for the fest
That little skinny tree shines brightly, completing the quest

Picture of the family for cards to be sent
Wrapping presents heartedly to present

Grandchild's programs we surely can't miss
Order the ham then under the mistletoe for a kiss

Holiday tunes carrying us on our way
Kids waiting for Santa to unpack his sleigh

Family gathered around on that glorious day
Getting ready to celebrate the birth of Jesus, hooray!

Brightly Lit

Massive ocean
More than grains of sand
Suddenly, a streak of light began
Wish of dreams transported by an unseen hand
Onto a cosmic caravan

Laying on my back
Cushioned by meadow green at midnight
Infinity captures my curiousness track
Questioning my insight
Map of ancient constellations revealing a mystical birthright

Romantic essence
Surrounds my soul
Manifestation of extreme peace
Voice you're not alone
Twinkling, gleaming, hand in hand when we take a stroll

Thermonuclear fusion of hydrogen into helium
Wisemen followed Polaris
Keeping their equilibrium
Bright light cast an aura
Like burning of magnesium

Sustaining life, hope, protection, and guidance
Representing faiths, David's proclaimed
Symbol for a child's rewarded game
Introducing the world's fame
Sports heroes and actors can be called by this name

Representing states and countries on a flag
Invasion vehicles painted with that tag
Six days of creation, with awe, and wonder
Staring up, experiencing all-rounder
Majestic encounter

Revealing a million miles afar
Illuminating a galaxy bazaar
Open celestial doorway
Of light far, far away
May the light be with you, they say

Free Flow

Let the words free flow
No rhyme, no reason, just let it go
Liking thoughts with no intention
Dribbling out with no suspension
Crafting and carving with no hesitation
Moving along the ocean floor
Actors huddled by the door
Outdoor fire pit cooking s'mores
Thinking, I used this line before
My rhythmic beat has no lesson
Pulsating within another dimension
Creating a bowl for sipping soup
Hot and spicy in a continuous loop
Ghostly fog engulfs the fjords
Unplugging cables, discern no more
Blind man sees, a deaf man speaks
Secrets of the puzzle's belief
Mirrors of my symmetry are discreet
Muscle and bone a force to reckon
Blockchains that transfer value in a second
The story of turning inside out
Completed the journey I turnabout
Free flow is spewing no doubt
That's what this is all about

12/19/21 **JK100**

Partners

Time has not forgotten
Adventurous fun
We unlocked
Waiting for my loved one
Divine patience rocks

Flowers given intimacy begun
Warming me up
Like the sun
Soulmates
Lottery won

Dancing, holding hands with devoted care
Making me laugh
Uniting a beautiful love affair
Encouraging new paragraphs
Adhering to the divine prayer map

Spiritual delight anointing refreshed
Together for others
Power in one flesh
Moves mountains, the cores uncovered
Miracles seen of healings discovered

Special gift
We have been given
Even in our misunderstandings
Harmony is driven
Grace allowed us to be forgiven

There's no other place
I would rather be
With my partner
In the hands of Godly unity
Dwelling in the house of the Lord for eternity

12/20/21 **JK101**

To Talk

Seems so simple
Hard for some
Took a long time
To naturally succumb
Before I knew
It was like a musical hum

Expressing my essence
Was a deep phenomenon
Especially speaking out loud
Sometimes I felt dumb
Answers, I found
Much deeper than scattered breadcrumbs

I confer all-day
Now it's engraved
Doesn't matter where or when
Always amazed
Awesome at the start of the day
Clears away the fleshly haze

Humble way of receiving
Guidance and comfort for the day
Clarity of the Word perceiving
The Rhema, it's not a cliché
Becomes supernaturally natural
Beautiful celestial stairway

We can intercede in asking
Most powerful tool lasting
Healing for anyone in need
In the human arsenal to decree
No commercials or casting
No cost, it's absolutely free

Valuable commodity of creation
Power you can't see
Ultimate enjoyable conversation
With the one who made me
Extremely precious narration
Of a necessary dialogue fulfilling every need

New Normal

Trying to stay away from this rhyme
Pressing in so hard it's a crime
Because of all the downtime
Words to express its only halftime

Wuhan's escape is still a mystery
Most of the planet fell to their knees
Over five million deaths and more to see
Not a slight breeze

Taken no warnings from the history lesson
Ventilators and masks weren't present
Hospitals overloaded with depression
Healthcare workers in torment

President unlocks restrictions to find a vaccine
Denounced as a liar, totally demeaned
Predecessor dreamed
He developed the machine

Dr. F appears every day approving mandates
Thousands of businesses go under losing the debate
Mask on, mask off, vaccine approved, its a date
Poke in the arm for most primates

Two shots better than one, a booster let's have some fun
Tragic and horrible for all who lost someone
Maneuvering through this new landscape, an end run
Affecting the loss of so many loved ones

Two new variances breaking through
Raging super villain Omicron mixed in with the flu
What villain before the holidays engineered this coup?
Mixing up this hideous stew

Hundreds of epidemiologist's different opinions and facts
Trust wearing thin foretold on the final contract
Out of misery a hope uprising of kindness unpacked
Supernaturally heading down the tracks

Can our future predict how long this will last?
Humanities outcome shattered like cracked glass
New normal, throwing a Hail Mary pass
Watching the goalposts moved on the evening newscast

12/23/21 **JK103**

Falling Flakes

It's a hypnotizing moment when the flakes fall
I feel like I'm in a crystal ball

You shake it up and watch it settle down
It's nature's time to dance around

With little wind, so softly float
So still and quiet, you can hear whispers spoke

They settled like hats on the pine green
Gathering like fancy coats, an incredible artist's dream

Before the plows and shovels are out
You witness a smooth sea of white all about

To read about it is not the same
If you've never felt or seen its fame

The famous flakes falling game

Get a front-row ticket, admissions free
It will dazzle your mind with supernatural serenity

Conflict

Golden strand
Woven through the tapestry by hand
Illuminating power to withstand
Revealing deep mysteries
Of the shepherd's history
Protecting his lamb

Shouting out to the crushing hoax
What I thought was a joke
Eliminating their power to provoke
Armed shield, my sword spoke
Receiving vision from the eye of the sparrow
Extinguishing destructive arrows

Combat against flesh and principalities
Rulers in the heavenlies
Maneuver through the battlefield
Wearing a helmet, breastplate concealed
Necessary weaponry
Escaping the enemy's death penalty

Raising heaven's flag
Symbol of eternity
Trumpet sounds the voice
Of forgiveness fearlessly
Those who do not surrender
Cast out of the symphony

Faith, necessary ingredient on holy street
Believing, a tight-fitting glove
Saving grace from above
Breaks the unbelief conceit
Supernatural power of love
Saving souls is now complete

Counselor Comforter

Flowing river, a waterfall
Vast ocean housed within
Drinking, living, water consuming all
Voices of angels begin to sing
Compass for direction, the anchor dug in

Knowledge to maneuver the landscape
Where to begin
Winds of counsel
Like the first day of spring
Intense fire refining the broken linchpin

Collapsed lung
Mended to breathe in, a peaceful wind
The voice is clear, tranquil, sincere
Under the wing's protective rim
At the cliff's edge, no more fear

Such comfort
To my fogless shape
Calling out my hesitation
Like a bee sting initiation
Opening all doors and windows to partake

Clears my path on the rocky road's courtship
So, I don't stumble and make a mistake
One of three, signet ring of the king's kinship
Completes my intimate relationship
Of my molded clay vessel remake

Partnership link expresses the essence
Pure love quakes
Heart mended by the master weaving loom
Multicolor strings bloom
Celebration of singing, dancing, darken storm breaks

Cherishing presence that awakes
Pouring down from the Kingdom for our sake
Supernatural gift to worship in faith
Healing for all our transgressions

Invited to the banquet table in the heavens
Sharing with the angels, the wedding cake

12/26/21 **JK106**

It's Not a Compromise

Holding on to the darkness
Of resentment and bitterness
Cut so hard into my humanity
Led me deep into the wilderness
Negative emotions filling insanity
The poisonous cup of wickedness

How can I see past the bookends?
Of genocidal slaughters, sickness
Justice for innocent to defend
Do I hold all accountable as a witness?
Is my soul condemned
Chained down to overwhelming deftness?

Requesting a pardon transaction
Will I remain blind?
Pursuing to remove allergic reaction
Purging my conscious mind
Voluntary effort, an unconditional action
May take a wealth of time

Being strangled by vengeance
I can hardly breathe
Anger scorching proctor
Screaming, it wants to seethe
Calling out to the heavenly doctor
Remove the wilting wreath

Apology is no resolve to heal the obscure
Perpetrators of murder and death
Repentance and redemption ensure
Forgiveness to clear my breath
Divine intervention, a cleansing miracle cure
Capturing my dissent from the river, Lethe

12/26/21 **JK107**

Delicious

Creamy brown
Covered over nuts and cashews
Not sure what I should choose
Too much gives me
Sugar blues

Once they were a nickel
Long time ago
Now they're a dollar and a half at the show
San Fran G-delli has an assortment of flavors
This I know

Four thousand-year history began in Mesoamerica
Cocoa bean was worshiped
Causes hysteria
Celebrate the union in France
Spread throughout the area

White, dark, milk, brute, bittersweet, semisweet
Liquor, Cocoa butter, lecithin, sugar, vanilla
Makes it complete
Mathez famous truffle
Located on the French street

My friends Hershey, Henry, Heath, Clark, Babe needed butter to release the stinger
Milky stayed with Charleston Rives who had to snicker at the Three Musketeers
Eat them up, don't linger
Employee pay day, kitty cat crunch the almond with joyful tears
Too many to count on my fingers

Little round fellows talking like a human cartel
Double initials in movies and commercials
Suck off the cover of duds you're left with caramel
Creating the most scrumptious parcels
Delectable treats shaped like a bell

Nature's gift, a tasty creamy marvel

A Deep Breath

Waiting in the airport line
Which password do I need to find?
The rotating circle boggles my mind

Stop and go light seems so long
Can they go any faster, move it along!
Express checkout line can't be wrong

Credit card, insurance, medical, a connection maze
TV app, phone provider, the computer kingpins, a nightmarish haze
Self-control, tolerance, it's burning up in a blaze

Children and grandchildren have taught me the most
Deep, inner reaction of composure, I must host
Loving marriage needs restraint and calmness or you're toast

Virtue if you have little or none
Keeping our humility equilibrium
If you can't tolerate or accept delay, it's no fun

Neutralizer to becoming angry or upset
Breeds gentleness, tranquility, so the beggar won't become a threat
Much-needed sounds of kindness, heard through our worldly headset

Gift or Curse

Adam and Eve were the first to conceive
Song of Solomon, a beautiful gift perceived
Pure heart a pure body, do some still believe

Monogamy, polyamory, adultery, which is thee?
Amorous action, it's opening the door with a key
Desire, stimulation, and arousal, a human delicacy

Tenderness of the flesh, a warmth connect, so heavenly
Excitement in reaching the summit, the peak, resolve, created divinely
Blending of our souls, sharing of our hearts, matched precisely

Sight, sounds, smells charming our innocence
Talk, touch, and sharing, fueling our indulgence
One together fulfilling our consciousness

Beautiful human trait for centuries dragged into the gutter
Consequences of pain creating a lot of clutter
Unwanted pregnancies, disease, slavery, power, and abuse, a broken rutter

Powerful divine gift sadly given to forsake
Change lives in an instant, a mother, a father to partake
For payment, profit, and pleasurable atrocities, a moral mistake

Pray for more mature fruit than decay
Commitment, trust, equality, honesty no delay
Intimacy of two, becoming one, a true expression of love, this way

Enivid Nommoc Esnes

Chopped up
Put in the blender, grind to pieces
Generating false press releases

Tomatoes with bananas
Drinking soup with a knife
Cutting steak with chopsticks in the cabana

Driving a car with no brakes
Diving two hundred feet off a cliff, into the lake
Adding a pound of yeast to the celebration cakes

Hiking into the wilderness without a backpack
Ice fishing on thin ice, no way back
Racing the one million dollar car on a dirt track

Losing the simple key to the lock
Thick, heavy oil added to water, a heart block
How many times do we have to be mocked?

Investigate the computer's algorithms
Pull the plug on all the sims
Black hole has arisen again

Constructing missiles, who really wins?
Have we moved on past that whim?
Power greed, money, politics, the new hymn

It's too disappointing I need to stop
Getting back to what's really sought
Our divine common thought

12/29/21 **JK111**

Finish Line

One hundred poems, riddles, and songs in one hundred days
Wasn't sure if I could go all the way

So much fun traveling through my imagination maze
Some serious, some fun, some even nutty, some with praise

Learned a lot on this colorful journey, the first recorded war
When soap and coal were discovered, the process opened many drawers

Some inner feelings I had to share
Had to release those wounds in prayer

Love telling stories and making people laugh
With rhymes and riddles, I hope some impressions will last

Inspirational reflective moments were such a gift
Like going to the top of the mountain on a chairlift

Expressing the seasons, grandchildren, children, family, and friends
My loving wife, I know our journey will never end

Politics, opinions, disease, sports, I gave it all a spin
The moon, the sun, the stars, behind the versus the sound of a violin

Birds, cats, and dogs, and even a dragon
Socks, earplugs, cars, and a circus wagon

Mouse, books, movies, music, got a haircut, went dancing
Words of inspiration from above about the kingdom advancing

Freedom, a soldier, chocolate, cakes, and cookies
Peace, memory, grief, and sadness, I no longer feel like a rookie

Falling flakes, a winter castle, fishing caught with a shiner
Where there's a design, I know there's a designer

That's the end of my first course now
We'll see what the new year brings, maybe 365 "How Now Brown Cows"

Roy Francis Krueger's
Poems

Thanks, Dad

I know these poems may be hard to read but I wanted to capture his actual writings instead of re-typing them.

So You Can't Talk! So What?

Drs took the voice box
Wife took the cash box
Can't find fault with Drs
Can't fight with the wife
So what do ye need a voice for
To go thru the rest of your life

There will always be paper & pencil
A typewriter, and the stewart
If you feel sorta lonely and need a lift
Just find a babe who cannot hear but can read lips

Sure there comes the time
When you'd like to tell someone off
Just like the days when you could talk
And no one listened to the stuff

~~Just be happy just be gay~~
~~There is always another day~~

Changing Times.

You stare at my graying hair
Pray tell me a color you would like
Perhaps black, brown or red
Maybe no hair at all instead.

The dome upon which this hair doth grow
I likened unto our four seasons
For me to change from what I have
I find no beneficial reason.

As likened unto sunshine was my hair
Of golden globe upon this dome was mine
And as I neared the age of mankind
I left the golden locks behind.

From spring of life to summer came
An age of care and growing
To keep a massive mop of hair upon the head
And keep all the bald spots from showing.

As summer passed on to the autumn
When nature changed to motley colors
So changed my hair as time passed on
As happened to so many others.

Now winter's here with snow and all pollution
My hair is colored like salt & pepper
I'm sure if you have a color to suggest
You might also have the proper solution.

As you read this
What are you hoping for
A word of love
  Then read no more

Perhaps a word of praise
  For things you've done
You shouldn't need that
  Cause your goal is ~~to it~~ really won

Maybe a word of ribbing
  From one who knows you well
Perhaps a bit of elderly guidance
  ~~Tell them all to go to hell~~
You've got a mind   To heed you
Perhaps only half a one

I got a conscience   Whatever
You've got one Too   Some thin
Mind says I'm crazy   You'll get
Does yours say so Too.   Before you

Don't listen to mine
I won't heed yours

They're dead! ~~Why~~
Why cry?
The good Book say
We're born to die.

Just how or when
Or even where
Should bring no fear
For God is there

Around, around a circle we go
What to do next, we do not know
Twenty four hours to get something done
But another 24 hours tomorrow will come

Mirror, mirror on the wall
Please tell me which is the sorest spot of all
Is it my throat so often cut
Or maybe at the other end — my butt

As you shine upon my face
Perhaps you'd say another place
Please tell me if you're sure
Which ever it is, this is a cure.

"Thanks", says the beggar boy, "for what?" --- *despair*
"Thanks", says the little boy and girl whose got. - *contentment*
"Thanks", says the cripple for the chair i ride, - *Appreciation*
"Thanks", says the blind man i have God by my side. *Resignation*.

    The end of the world comes not when you die for there is another one ~~here~~ beyond. You paid the rent far in advance while you were living for the mansion you enter after death. Where you go there is no housing shortage, taxes, race trouble, or war or elections. The "President" was not elected ~~for~~ *AND* He was always there.

    So if you plan to go to a place after you are tired of living down here among all the turmoil, prepare ahead of time so you won't find yourself in a hell of a ~~palce~~ *PLACE*,

> No promises or threats
> No apologies or ~~regs~~ regrets
> For every day that goes God's way
> I'm thankful and will stop to pray

SECTION

Come Dasher, come Blitzen
And all you other deers
We're almost rid of all this junk
Until the coming year

He didn't know I saw him
As he moved around
But then who'd expect to see him
With his bag laying on the ground.

I'm sure he was real tired
And his journey was quite slow
Cause the place where at we live
There isn't any snow.

> I asked God for help and He gave me help. After He helped me I thanked Him. After thanking Him I prayed to God that He would help me remember what help he gave me.

Hop along Bunny
And don't be gunny
We know what's on your mind
Your mate's a-waiting impatiently
Among the chestnut and the pine
We know when Easter Sunday comes around
There'll be many more of your kind

If my boy was a dissenter
You ask what I would do?
I'd listen to that college boy
And maybe be one too.

I'd bridge the gap of age and youth
And weigh the cons and pros
For when it comes down to the war
He's the one that has to go.

He ~~says we don't belong in Vietnam~~
~~to that I must agree~~
But no matter why he don't agree
What's goin' on in this big country
He can't be having too much fun
Cause he ain't ~~writin~~ askin' for money.

About the Author

Jeffrey Krueger was born in Milwaukee, Wisconsin, 1952. He grew up on the Northside of Milwaukee in the housing project known as Westlawn. After his parents divorced at the age of eleven, he moved into his grandmother's home in Wauwatosa, a suburb of Milwaukee and graduated from Wauwatosa East High in 1970. Continuing his studies attending Layton School of Fine Arts, Milwaukee; University of Milwaukee, Wisconsin; and the University of Minnesota, Minneapolis; spanning the years from 1970–1978.

He has been involved in the entertainment business for over fifty years. After arriving back from the Woodstock festival in 1969, he produced his first outdoor concert in 1970.

In the late '70s and early '80s, he was lead singer of the music group, the American Pilots, writing and producing the demo LP, Heart Notes. For a short time, he became an entertainment consultant in the Twin Cities area, producing performances of Chuck Berry, Eddie Money, Savoy Brown, Traffic, Todd Rundgren, The Baby's, Ricky Nelson, Tommy James & the Shondells, Kiki Dee, Hall & Oates, Peter Tosh, Herman's Hermit and Poco.

In 1983, he founded the country music festival WE Fest, Detroit Lakes, Minnesota, one of the largest festivals in the nation. For twenty-eight years, he was at the helm as president of the WE Fest until his semi-retirement in 2010. He produced shows of the *who's who in country music, to just mention a few: Dolly Parton, Johnny Cash, Willie Nelson, Waylon Jennings, Tim McGraw, Kenny Chesney, Miranda Lambert, Kid Rock, Keith Urban, Carrie Underwood, George Strait, Little Big Town, Brad Paisley, Blake Sheldon, Eric Church, Rascal Flatts, and Taylor Swift.*

After rededicating his life to his Christian faith at a Promise Keepers event in Minneapolis in August 1997, he launched a Christian festival called Spirit Fest. It included six stages and over thirty musical acts and speakers per day, including artists Michael W. Smith, Amy Grant, Steven Curtis Chapman, Third Day, Newsboys, Point of Grace, Skillet, Big Daddy Weave, Delirious, Phil Driscoll, Ragamuffin Band, 4Him, and a host of others.

He created a fundraiser called the Family Needs Fund, a nonprofit organization. It was designed and dedicated to assisting the crisis and circumstantial needs of families. For the last eighteen years, the charity has been active in helping families with their basic needs and continues today. In addition, he produced two live musical worship CDs of the Power of God Band, "Delivered" and "POG Live." Both CDs were sold, being utilized as a fundraiser to raise funds for families in need. All the proceeds were donated to the FNF charity.

He shared his written testimony on how God saved his life, healing him from the addiction to drugs and his battle with depression. He witnessed the healing power of the Holy Spirit, guiding him throughout his life, and is reflected in some of his poems.

During his retirement, he consulted a small Christian music festival, called Hope Fest, a fundraiser for the homeless, hungry, and lost. For the last thirty-six years, he has been a devoted husband, father, and grandfather to four children and nine grandchildren. He defeated cancer with God's healing power, became a full-time farmer at Hardwood Hills Vineyard, reclaimed wood-furniture-maker, and inventor of E-Z Stack, e-zstack.com.

He began exploring writing to challenge himself in 2004 to help overcome his Dyslexic learning disorder. He finished his first writing, a screenplay called The Maestro, *in 2009. He continued writing his autobiography,* Cause-and-Effect: A Life's Journey.

He started writing Dad's 100 Poems, Riddles, and Songs in 100 Days *on September 20, 2021, finishing on December 29, 2021. His poems range from sometimes silly subjects a mouse, socks circus, balloons, clouds, to more serious reflections of his life, loss of a loved one, addiction, abuse, depression, divorce, also recording daily moments of the surroundings and habitat around him. Some commentary on certain subjects' freedom, sports, war, and the environment. Many of his poems are also a reflection of his Judeo-Christian faith, believing in the power of prayer and the healing power of God's Holy Spirit.*

Proceeds from the sale of *Dad's 100 Poems, Riddles, and Songs in 100 Days* are donated to the Family Needs Fund, a charity to help families in need.